ICE CREAM
GALORE

ICE CREAM
GALORE

CAROLINE BARTY

spruce

An Hachette UK Company

First published in Great Britain in 2009
by Spruce, a division of
Octopus Publishing Group Ltd
2–4 Heron Quays, London E14 4JP
www.octopusbooks.co.uk
www.octopusbooksusa.com

Distributed in the U.S. and Canada for
Octopus Books USA
c/- Hachette Book Group USA
237 Park Avenue
New York NY 10017.

ISBN 13 978-1-84601-323-2
ISBN 10 1-84601-323-2

A CIP catalog record of this book is available
from the Library of Congress.

Printed and bound in China

10 9 8 7 6 5 4 3 2 1

Many thanks to the following suppliers who
loaned us their marvellous ice cream makers
for the book:
Cuisinart – readers can call Cuisinart on
0044 (0) 870 240 6902 for further
information or visit www.cuisinart.co.uk
Magimix – readers can call Magimix
Customer Care 0044 (0)1483 427411 for
futher information or visit www.magimix.com

This book contains the opinions and ideas of
the author. It is intended to provide helpful
and informative material on the subjects
addressed in this book and is sold with the
understanding that the author and publisher
are not engaged in rendering any kind of
personal professional services in this book.
The author and publisher disclaim all
responsibility for any liability, loss, or risk,
personal or otherwise, which is incurred as
a consequence, directly or indirectly, of the
use and application of any of the contents
of this book.

The Food and Drug Administration advises
that eggs should not be consumed raw. This
book contains some dishes made with raw
eggs. It is prudent for more vulnerable people,
such as pregnant or nursing mothers, invalids,
the elderly, babies, and young children to
avoid uncooked or lightly cooked dishes
made with eggs.

Photography: Janine Hosegood
Food Styling: Jennie Shapter
Page Layout: Balley Design Limited

CONTENTS

INTRODUCTION

There can be few foods that enjoy the universal popularity of ice cream. We may not all like the same flavors but ask anyone and they will always be able to tell you their favorite ice cream. Times have moved on from the days when the holy trinity of vanilla, chocolate, and strawberry were the only flavors on offer. When it comes to making your own, there is now a mind-boggling array to choose from and to inspire you.

The biggest benefit of homemade ice creams is that you know exactly what goes into each one—not an e number or added fat in sight. This, of course, means they won't last as long as commercial brands, but a homemade ice is so delicious that it won't stay in the freezer for long, although it will keep for about two months. Also, unless you have access to industrial-size churning machines you can't make a huge quantity at one batch. On average, most machines make about 4 cups at a time.

TYPES OF ICES & ICE CREAMS

Whether you prefer creamy ice creams or the cleaner, refreshing flavors of sorbets and granitas, ices must rate as one of the most popular desserts of all time. Not all of them need to be calorie-laden treats—you can find ices to suit most dietary needs, from eggless to dairy-free examples (see pages 150–165).

★ ICE CREAMS ★

There is always a lively debate as to which country makes the best ice cream. Some say the Italian ice creams take first prize for quality as their ices, which are made with more eggs and just milk, have a superior texture and cleaner flavor, whereas others prefer the softer, creamier ices that are made in France, which have a higher ratio of cream to milk and eggs. Americans, too, favor a sweet, rich and creamy ice cream.

Most of the recipe methods in this book include instructions for making ice cream in a machine, but do not think that you cannot make ice cream without a machine—you just have to accept that the finished texture will not be as smooth and creamy. You do, however, need a food processor to break down the ice crystals. When a recipe states "churn and freeze," simply freeze the ice until it is just hard, then spoon it into the food processor and process for a few seconds until sloppy. Return to the container and freeze until hard. If the ice has added bits, such as raisins and chocolate chips etc., then these need to be incorporated after the processing as you want to retain their texture.

Homemade ices are harder than commercial brands and need 10–15 minutes at room temperature to soften before serving. Some lower-fat varieties may require a little longer.

★ SORBETS ★

Sorbets or water ices have a sugar syrup base to which a juice or fruit puree is added. The mixture is then churned and sometimes has the addition of an egg white, which gives a lovely, light, slightly frothy texture.

As with the ice creams, an ice-cream maker (sometimes called a sorbetière) produces the smoothest-textured sorbets. If you don't have an ice-cream maker, just follow the principles of ice-cream making. Freeze the liquid until just hard, then spoon it into a food processor and process until smooth. Spoon it into the container again and continue to freeze until hard. In general, I found my ice-cream maker churned a sorbet to almost frozen, so you could serve it almost at once, but if making by hand, it will take longer to harden, about 5–6 hours. Before serving sorbets or sherbets (see page 10), leave at room temperature for 5–10 minutes, or until you can easily scoop.

★ SPOOMS ★

These are similar to the egg-white enriched sorbet but a little extra sugar is added to the beaten egg whites, like an uncooked meringue base, to give a light, frothy texture. If you don't have an ice-cream maker and wish to make Strawberry Spoom (see pages 112–113), follow the instructions above for making the sorbet by hand. Spooms need to be left at room temperature for about 5 minutes before serving.

★ SHERBETS ★

Many countries have their own version of sherbet so this type of frozen dessert is harder to define. The name is said to have derived from an Arab word meaning a cold sweet drink. Usually it is a sorbet with a touch of added cream or milk. Sherbets are more like sorbets in texture but they have a creamier flavor due to the added dairy products. If you are making a sherbet without an ice-cream maker, proceed in the same way as for the ice creams and sorbets.

★ PARFAITS OR SEMIFREDDOS ★

Parfaits or, as the Italians call them, semifreddos (literally half-chilled) are lighter and more delicate than ice creams due to the air incorporated into the egg yolks and cream when whipped. They are a more delicate and easy alternative to classic churned ice creams. As the mixture is not churned and the ice crystals don't need to be broken down, they are a great way to start making your own frozen ices because the costly investment in an ice-cream maker is not required. Once made, simply freeze and serve straight from the freezer.

As parfaits (or semifreddos) may be served direct from the freezer, they can be poured into glasses or ramekins ready for the table. I use chunky tumblers to serve parfaits as they store easily in the freezer and won't shatter. Alternatively, you could spoon the parfait into suitable freezer containers (small foil trays come in handy here), freeze and then serve in scoops in more delicate glasses. Parfaits also make excellent fillings for frozen bombes as their softer texture complements a harder ice-cream shell.

The classic method to make a parfait is from an Italian meringue base. That is sugar syrup boiled to firm ball stage (257°F), which is poured over stiffly

beaten eggs. The mixture is then beaten until cold. However, a certain degree of skill is required and quite frankly it doesn't taste any different to the easy method of combining beaten egg yolks, sugar, and cream. The key to a good parfait is to beat the egg yolks with the sugar until they have almost tripled in size. You can do this over a pan of barely simmering water (as you would to make a hollandaise sauce or a zabaglione), but as long as you have some good electric beaters, it is not important.

STORAGE

Homemade ices do not keep as well as store-bought ones and they tend to start to spoil after two months in a domestic freezer. Sorbets and granitas may be frozen a little longer as the texture is compromised less by the formation of ice crystals. As stated at the front of this book, pregnant women, the elderly, and those with immune-deficient health problems should all avoid eating food containing raw eggs.

★ GRANITAS ★

A granita is an Italian frozen water ice that has not been churned. Instead, it is beaten with a fork to produce a grainy ice. It is best to freeze the liquid in a wide, shallow container as it freezes more quickly and it is easier to scrape the ice crystals from around the edges. The general rule is that granitas need to be stirred with a fork every 30–40 minutes for 4–5 hours, and they are ready to be served when just hard. They can be frozen, but a bit of texture may be lost in the process. Due to its texture, granita is usually piled into a glass for serving (if it has frozen solid, you may need to let it stand at room temperature before scraping).

★ FREEZING & SETTING TIMES ★

The setting time (that is, the freezing time) for ice creams varies, depending on whether you use an ice-cream machine or make ice cream by hand. As an ice-cream machine churns the ice so that it is almost frozen, it only takes about 1 hour to set hard, but if you are making ice cream by hand, it takes longer— about 4–5 hours depending on the freezer (small compartment freezers may take longer).

The savory ices in this book won't take as long to freeze as the sweet flavors as they are smaller in quantity and in the ice-cream maker they tend to be almost frozen hard.

★ SERVING ICE CREAM ★

You need to think a little ahead when serving homemade ices (ice creams, in particular) as they need between 10–15 minutes at room temperature, or as long as it takes to insert a spoon or scoop easily. Ices with a low-fat content tend to be harder. If the ice cream thaws completely, it is unfortunate but it must be thrown away or the bacteria will start to multiply.

★ CHOCOLATE CARAQUE ★

Another name for big chocolate curls. Melt 4–5 ounces chocolate and pour over a marble slab. Allow it to harden. It needs to be hard but not completely set. At a 45° angle to the surface draw the blade of a small sharp knife across the chocolate, away from the body. Turn the point of the knife a little as if you are about to trace a circle. The chocolate should form long curls. It is crucial to get the correct angle of the blade and also that the chocolate is at the right temperature. Too hot and the curls will collapse and too cold, that is set, and the chocolate will form shards rather than curls.

★ CHOCOLATE LEAVES ★

Firstly you will need the leaves of a nontoxic plant. Rose and bay leaves are best as they have well-defined veins. Wash the leaves and allow to dry completely. Melt the chocolate and paint the underside of the leaves with chocolate. Allow to harden and set, then carefully peel off the leaves.

EQUIPMENT

In general, if you are a keen cook and have a well-equipped kitchen you will already have everything you need to make your own ice cream. Basic necessities include cutting boards, a range of different-size saucepans, knives, graters, sieves, and spoons.

★ GLASSES ★

So long as they are not fine or thin, and there is not a sudden change of temperature, most glasses can be safely frozen (see also Parfaits, page 10).

★ ICE-CREAM SCOOPS ★

On the whole, homemade ices freeze harder than commercial ones and so a good solid ice-cream scoop can come in handy for serving. The oval, quenelle-shaped scoops give a more restaurant-style shape, but there is nothing wrong with the old-fashioned ball variety.

★ FREEZER CONTAINERS ★

I like to keep a selection of these especially for ice cream as they are not tainted with the smells of other foodstuffs. A secure lid is useful—you don't want the ice cream to spill all over the freezer. For sealing, I also use foil. Always label any batch with a note of the flavor and the date the ice was made.

★ WOODEN SPOONS ★

In the same way that I keep containers especially for ices, I like to reserve two or three wooden spoons for making sweet recipes as the wood soaks up strong, savory flavors. Metal spoons can ruin the surfaces of nonstick pans and also heat up to dangerous levels.

★ SPATULAS ★

Keep a selection of these on hand to stir and scrape every last drop of mixture from saucepans and bowls.

★ HEAT-DIFFUSING MAT ★

If you are not confident when it comes to making custards, then a heat-diffusing mat (for powerful gas burners) is helpful—the heat becomes less powerful and therefore the custard will be less likely to curdle.

★ MOLDS ★

Wonderfully wacky molds are available in catalogs, specialty stores, and via the Internet, but a good old-fashioned popsicle mold is always useful and a great way to get children involved in cooking. The recipes in the Frosted Delights chapter (see pages 88–133) make good popsicles as they freeze hard and some of the recipes for sorbets that don't include egg whites can also be used for making shaped ices.

I don't favor intricate, fancy-shaped molds as the ice cream tends to melt and lose its shape on unmolding but little ramekins, deep cake pans, etc. make fine molds. Hollowed-out oranges and lemons are a fun way to present ices, too. You can also jazz up the look with toasted chopped nuts, crushed cookies, silver dragées, or chocolate curls, and if you want to go retro, try some candy sprinkles.

★ SAUCEPANS ★

A selection of good thick-based, nonstick saucepans is vital for the custard-making stage of ices as the custard is less likely to catch and burn or curdle.

★ ICE-CREAM MAKERS ★

If you are serious about making your own ices and want to do so on a regular basis, there is no alternative but to invest in a good-quality ice-cream maker. The best (and most expensive, naturally) are the machines that churn and freeze at the same time (transfer to freezerproof containers, if not using straightaway)[3]. There is no question that they do result in the best ice cream.

Also available are Ice cream machines with removeable bowls that you place in the freezer for a few hours ahead of actually making the ice cream or sorbet[1&2]. The key difference between this machine and the "churn and freeze" machine is that you can only make one batch of ice cream at a time, as you need to re-freeze the bowl.

★ EQUIPMENT FOR MAKING ICE CREAM WITHOUT AN ICE-CREAM MAKER ★

Similarly to making bread, many people think that ice-cream making is a long and complicated process, but this could not be further from the truth. You do not need special gadgets or hi-tech equipment—my grandmother used to make ices with the most basic equipment.

★ ELECTRIC BEATER ★

An electric beater, hand-held or a processor with a balloon whisk attachment, is vital to incorporate air into the base mixture, especially in parfaits.

★ FOOD PROCESSOR & MIX MASTER ★

If you don't have an ice-cream maker, then a food processor is essential—you need to break down the ice crystals rapidly before the almost-frozen ice starts to melt and ruin. Alternatively, you can use your mix master on maximum speed.

INGREDIENTS

As with all cooking, the finer the ingredients you use, the better the finished product and ice cream is no exception. Buy the best you can afford, and with all fruit and vegetables, look for the juiciest, ripest examples. Always check spices and nuts that have been stored to see that they are still in date before using.

★ EGGS ★

I am without compromise on this subject. The eggs used in ices must be free-range and preferably organic. This is not just a matter of taste but of responsible and ethical animal husbandry. These vary a little more in size than battery eggs but try to buy large eggs.

If you have a lot of leftover egg whites, make them into meringues and pavlovas. Also, if you do not want to use them immediately, they freeze very well. Simply store in freezer bags or small containers, labeled with the date and the amount of egg whites and then freeze for up to 6 months. Defrost thoroughly before use.

★ MILK ★

Preferably whole for a slightly softer-textured ice cream, but lowfat will do if you are watching your weight.

★ CREAM ★

I prefer to use whipping cream in ice-cream recipes as heavy cream can result in a more cloying texture, but you can experiment to find your favorite.

★ YOGURT ★

The whole milk varieties give a slightly better finished flavor and texture. Yogurt-based ices are fresh and zingy-tasting. They lack the richness and smoothness of cream and custard-based ices, but are delicious nonetheless.

★ CRÈME FRAÎCHE ★

A slightly soured thick cream that can be heated, crème fraîche gives a tangy fresh flavor to ice creams. The whole milk varieties work best. Again, this is a matter of texture as using lowfat varieties results in a lack of smoothness in the finished ice cream. Crème fraîche can be found in specialty stores.

★ SOY MILK & YOGURT ★

For the lactose-intolerant and vegans these are vital ingredients that can be made into delicious ices. Soy milk and yogurt on its own can be an acquired taste, but mixed with fruit and frozen, this is a great way to enjoy ice cream. Even if you are without any food intolerances, the health benefits of soy protein and yogurt are excellent.

★ VANILLA BEANS & VANILLA EXTRACT ★

Vanilla beans should be squidgy and moist when purchased. They add a depth of flavor and a subtle, grainy texture to ices. Always look for pure vanilla extract, not vanilla flavoring, which has an unpleasant artificial taste.

★ CHOCOLATE ★

In most recipes the cocoa solid content is specified and 50–70% generally gives the densest flavor. Whether you buy organic is a matter of taste. I don't think it has a finer flavor, but experiment with varieties to find your favorite. Keep chocolate in a cool, dry place. Sudden changes in temperature result in a pale bloom forming on the chocolate.

To make chocolate decorations, melt a little chocolate and drizzle onto nonstick waxd paper. Peel off the designs when hard. For chocolate curls, spread melted chocolate onto a marble slab in a thin, even layer. Allow to harden, then scrape over the surface with a sharp knife angled at 40–45° until curls are formed. Refrigerate immediately to prevent melting.

★ SUGAR ★

Superfine sugar is best as it dissolves more quickly. Fructose (from health food stores and supermarkets) works well in the fruit recipes as it brings out the flavor of fresh fruit. The balance of sugar is vital in ices—too much sugar prevents the ice from freezing correctly, while not enough results in an unpleasant hardness and lack of good texture.

★ ALCOHOL ★

Alcohol should be used sparingly in ices as it can impair the freezing process, leaving you with a slushy, unfrozen ice. It is also unpleasant to taste a lot of raw alcohol in ices. Recipes using alcohol and also those containing caffeine are of course unsuitable for children.

★ FROSTED DECORATIONS ★

To frost grapes, dip washed, seedless white grapes in lightly beaten egg white and roll in superfine sugar. Dust off the excess sugar and leave until hard. Small violets, primrose flowers, and rose petals can be treated in the same way.

RICH & CREAMY
ICE CREAMS

CLASSIC VANILLA ICE CREAM

Homemade vanilla ice cream can beat all other flavors hands-down. The key is to use fresh vanilla beans—even a good extract does not carry the same flavor as a bean.

SERVES 4–6

2 fat vanilla beans
1¼ cups milk
¾ cup whipping cream
5 egg yolks
½ cup superfine sugar

1. Use a sharp knife to cut down the middle of each vanilla bean lengthwise and scrape the seeds into a saucepan. Add the beans and pour in the milk and cream. Slowly bring to a boil, then remove and allow to infuse for 5 minutes. Remove the beans (see tip).

2. Beat the egg yolks with the superfine sugar until light and fluffy and then pour over the vanilla milk.

3. Return to the pan and stir over a gentle heat until the mixture is thick enough to coat the back of a spoon. Allow to cool, then churn in an ice-cream maker according to the manufacturer's instructions until set (thick) and then spoon into a suitable freezing container and freeze until hard (almost at once if making in a machine, but 5–6 hours if making by hand).

4. Soften at room temperature, 10–15 minutes, before serving.

ICE-CREAM TIP

Wash the beans really well, pat dry with paper towels or allow to dry at room temperature and then place in a jar of superfine sugar. They will infuse the sugar with a mild vanilla flavor. You can use the sugar in most cake and dessert recipes that call for sugar and vanilla flavoring. Equally, the vanilla sugar could be sprinkled over cakes, cookies or pancakes.

BASIC CHOCOLATE ICE CREAM

Still as delicious as the Rich Chocolate Ice Cream (see page 26) but prepared in a flash and less intensely flavored. For a much milder taste, use a good-quality milk chocolate.

SERVES 4–6

1¼ cups whipping cream
¾ cup milk
4oz roughly chopped bittersweet chocolate (50% cocoa solids)
1¼ cups condensed milk

1. Put the cream, milk, and chocolate in a saucepan and stir over a low heat until the chocolate has melted and the mixture is smooth.

2. Remove the saucepan from the heat and stir in the condensed milk. Allow to cool completely.

3. Churn in an ice-cream maker according to the manufacturer's instructions until set (thick) and then spoon into a suitable freezing container and freeze until hard (almost at once if making in a machine, but 5–6 hours if making by hand).

4. Soften at room temperature, 10–15 minutes, before serving.

RICH CHOCOLATE ICE CREAM

To my mind, the best chocolate ice cream with an intense flavor and velvety texture. It's one for the grownups rather than children.

SERVES 4–6

1¼ cups milk
1 teaspoon vanilla extract
⅔ cup finely chopped bittersweet chocolate (70% cocoa solids)
4 egg yolks
½ cup superfine sugar
1 cup whipping cream

1. Put the milk and vanilla extract in a saucepan and bring to a boil. Sprinkle with the chopped chocolate and leave for 10 minutes. Stir until the mixture is smooth and the chocolate has melted.

2. Beat the egg yolks with the superfine sugar until light and fluffy. Pour the chocolate mixture over the eggs and then pour back the combined mixture into the pan. Stir over a gentle heat until the mixture is thick enough to coat the back of a spoon. Allow to cool.

3. Very lightly whip the cream and stir into the cooled chocolate. Churn in an ice-cream maker according to the manufacturer's instructions until the ice cream is on the point of setting (thick) and then spoon into a suitable freezing container and freeze until hard (almost at once if making in a machine, but 5–6 hours if making by hand).

4. Soften at room temperature, 10–15 minutes, before serving.

WHITE CHOCOLATE ICE CREAM

Using ready-made fresh custard means this ice cream can be made in a matter of minutes.

SERVES 4–6

²/₃ cup roughly chopped white chocolate
1¼ cups whipping cream
²/₃ cup milk
2 teaspoons vanilla extract
1 cup ready-made fresh custard

1. Put the white chocolate in a saucepan with the cream, milk, and vanilla extract. Stir over a low heat until the chocolate has melted and the mixture is smooth.

2. Remove from the heat and allow to cool a little before stirring in the custard. Cool completely.

3. Churn in an ice-cream maker according to the manufacturer's instructions until set (thick) and then spoon into a suitable freezing container and freeze until hard (almost at once if making in a machine, but 5–6 hours if making by hand).

4. Soften at room temperature, 10–15 minutes, before serving.

ICE CREAM TIP
Add some white chocolate chips to the custard before churning to give the ice cream a lovely crunch.

SALTED ALMOND & MILK CHOCOLATE ICE CREAM

I buy a delicious candy bar made by Côte d'Or but you can also use an ordinary bar of nutty milk chocolate and add a pinch of salt to the custard to make this ice cream.

SERVES 4–6

7oz bar caramelized salted almond
    and milk chocolate
1 cup whipping cream
⅔ cup milk
1¼ cups ready-made fresh custard

1. Break the chocolate up into cubes and put in a saucepan with the cream and milk. Stir over a low heat until the chocolate has melted.

2. Remove from the heat and then allow to cool a little before stirring in the custard. Cool completely.

3. Churn in an ice-cream maker according to the manufacturer's instructions until set (thick) and then spoon into a suitable freezing container and freeze until hard (almost at once if making in a machine, but 5–6 hours if making by hand).

4. Soften at room temperature, 10–15 minutes, before serving.

PEANUT BRITTLE ICE CREAM

You can make the peanut brittle well ahead of time and store it in an airtight container for 2 to 3 weeks. Serve this ice cream with extra brittle on top.

SERVES 4–6

1¾ cups milk
⅔ cup cream
3 egg yolks
½ cup superfine sugar

FOR THE PEANUT BRITTLE

⅓ superfine sugar
6 tablespoons light corn syrup
½ cup unsalted peanuts
1 tablespoon unsalted butter
½ teaspoon baking soda

ICE-CREAM TIP

For a honeycomb alternative, follow the instructions for peanut brittle but omit the peanuts. Break up the honeycomb, stir into the custard, and churn in the usual way.

1. To make the peanut brittle, first oil a 10 x 14 inch jelly roll pan. Place the sugar and corn syrup in a large, heavy saucepan and bring to a boil, stirring.

2. When the temperature has reached 275°F, add the peanuts and butter. Continue to cook until the temperature reaches 305°F. Remove from the heat and add the baking soda. Pour into the prepared pan and leave until cold and hard, then tap the peanut brittle into pieces with a small hammer.

3. Put the milk and cream into a saucepan and bring to a boil.

4. Beat the egg yolks and sugar until light and fluffy, then pour over the hot milk and cream. Return to the pan and stir over a gentle heat until the mixture is thick enough to coat the back of a spoon. Remove from the heat and cool completely.

5. Finely chop the peanut brittle and stir into the custard. Churn in an ice-cream maker according to the manufacturer's instructions until set (thick) and then spoon into a suitable freezing container and freeze until hard (almost at once if making by machine, but 5–6 hours if making by hand).

6. Soften at room temperature, 10–15 minutes, before serving.

COFFEE ICE CREAM

This is a real coffee-lover's ice cream. Strong and full of flavor, it
is great served with a splash of chocolate sauce and whipped cream.

SERVES 4–6

1½ cups milk
1 cup whipping cream
2 heaping tablespoons ground coffee
5 egg yolks
⅔ cup superfine sugar

1. Put the milk, cream, and ground coffee in a saucepan and slowly bring to boiling point. Remove from the heat and allow to infuse for 20 minutes.

2. Put the egg yolks and sugar into a bowl and beat until light and fluffy. Strain the coffee milk through a sieve lined with a piece of cheesecloth, then pour over the egg mixture and stir to combine.

3. Return to a clean pan and gently heat, stirring, until the mixture is thick enough to coat the back of a spoon. Allow to get cold, then churn in an ice-cream maker according to the manufacturer's instructions until set (thick). Spoon into a suitable freezing container and freeze until hard (almost at once if making in a machine, but 5–6 hours if making by hand).

4. Soften at room temperature, 10–15 minutes, before serving.

ICE-CREAM TIP
*For a pretty decoration, top
scoops of coffee ice cream
with 2–3 chocolate-coated
espresso beans.*

COOKIE-DOUGH ICE CREAM

This is an absolute favorite with children, who love to eat the raw cookie dough. You can find cookie dough in the ready-made pastry section in most supermarkets.

SERVES 4–6

1¼ cups milk
¾ cup whipping cream
5 egg yolks
½ cup superfine sugar
2 teaspoons vanilla extract
½oz ready-made chocolate-chip cookie dough, finely chopped

1. In a saucepan bring the milk and cream to a boil. Meanwhile, beat together the egg yolks, sugar, and vanilla extract until light and fluffy.

2. Pour over the hot milk and cream, then mix to combine. Return the liquid to the pan and stir over a gentle heat until the mixture coats the back of a spoon. Remove from the heat and allow to cool.

3. Churn in an ice-cream maker according to the manufacturer's instructions until the ice cream just holds its shape. Fold in the chopped cookie dough and pour into a suitable freezing container. Freeze until hard (almost at once if making in a machine, but 5–6 hours if making by hand).

4. Soften at room temperature, 10–15 minutes, before serving.

DOUBLE CHOC-CHIP ICE CREAM

Use semisweet or white chocolate chips, or a mixture of both. If you like a darker, richer chocolate flavor, choose a chocolate with 70% cocoa solids. Less cocoa solids gives a lighter flavor, which children tend to prefer.

SERVES 4

1½ cups milk

6 tablespoons whipping cream

⅔ cup sweetened condensed milk

½ cup roughly chopped bittersweet chocolate (50–70% cocoa solids)

3 egg yolks

¼ cup superfine sugar

⅓ cup chocolate chips

1. Put the milk, cream, condensed milk, and chocolate in a saucepan. Stir over a gentle heat until the chocolate has melted.

2. Beat the egg yolks and sugar until light and fluffy, then pour over the chocolate milk. Return to the pan and stir over a gentle heat until the mixture thickens just enough to coat the back of a spoon. Set aside and allow to cool completely.

3. Churn in an ice-cream maker according to the manufacturer's instructions until the ice cream is on the point of setting, then scrape into a bowl and stir in the chocolate chips. Spoon into a suitable freezing container and freeze until hard (almost at once if making in a machine, but 5–6 hours if making by hand).

4. Soften at room temperature, 10–15 minutes, before serving.

MALTED CHOCOLATE ICE CREAM

Chocolate-coated honeycomb balls lend a satisfying crunch to this delicious ice cream.

SERVES 4–6

1½ cups milk

1¼ cups whipping cream

⅔ cup roughly chopped plain chocolate (50% cocoa solids)

4 egg yolks

⅓ cup superfine sugar

4 heaping tablespoons malted drink powder

⅓ cup roughly crushed malt balls

1. Put the milk, cream, and chopped chocolate into a saucepan. Stir over a gentle heat until the chocolate melts. Keep on a low heat while you beat the egg yolks with the sugar until light and fluffy.

2. Stir the malted drink powder into the beaten egg mixture. Pour over the hot chocolate milk and stir well.

3. Return to the pan and stir over a gentle heat until the mixture thickens (often there is a thickening agent in the drink powder so the custard will be slightly thicker than usual). Remove from the heat and allow to cool completely.

4. Churn in an ice-cream maker according to the manufacturer's instructions until set (thick), then stir in the crushed chocolate-coated malt balls. Spoon into a suitable freezing container and freeze until hard (almost at once if making in a machine, but 5–6 hours if making by hand).

5. Soften at room temperature, 10–15 minutes, before serving.

MINT CHOCOLATE ICE CREAM

Gooey fondant chocolate mints have the best texture and flavor but you can use bitter mints. Adjust the sugar if the custard lacks sweetness. Serve in a bowl decorated with fresh mint sprigs.

SERVES 4–6

10oz mint chocolate fondants
1¼ cups milk
1¼ cups whipping cream
1¼ cups ready-made fresh custard

1. Arrange the chocolate mints in the base of a large heatproof bowl.

2. Bring the milk and cream to a boil and pour over the mints. Stir until the chocolate mints have melted. Cool completely.

3. Stir in the custard, transfer to an ice-cream maker, and churn according to the manufacturer's instructions until set (thick) and then spoon into a suitable freezing container and freeze until hard (almost at once if making in a machine, but 5–6 hours if making by hand).

4. Soften at room temperature, 10–15 minutes, before serving.

CREAM CHEESECAKE ICE CREAM

This ice cream really does taste like frozen cheesecake. With their hint of saltiness, graham crackers contrast well with the creaminess of the ice, but you can also use gingersnaps.

SERVES 4–6

¾ cup roughly crushed graham crackers (see tip)
1 tablespoon melted butter
1 cup cream cheese
⅔ cup superfine sugar
2 teaspoons vanilla extract
1¼ cups ready-made fresh custard
⅔ cup whipping cream

1. Put the crushed crackers in a heatproof bowl and stir in the melted butter. Set aside to harden slightly.

2. Meanwhile, beat the cream cheese with the sugar and vanilla extract until smooth. Stir in the custard and whipping cream, then chill for 10 minutes.

3. Churn in an ice-cream maker according to the manufacturer's instructions until just set (thick) and then stir in the crackers. Spoon into a suitable freezing container and freeze until hard (almost at once if making in a machine, but 5–6 hours if making by hand).

4. Soften at room temperature, 10–15 minutes, before serving.

ICE-CREAM TIP
The easiest way to crush the crackers is to place them in a plastic bag. Seal and tap lightly with a rolling pin.

CINNAMON ICE CREAM

I like to serve this with a treacle tart or syrup sponge as the cinnamon complements and cuts through the sweetness of the ice cream.

SERVES 4–6

1¾ cups milk
⅔ cup whipping cream
2 cinnamon sticks
4 egg yolks
½ cup superfine sugar
1 teaspoon ground cinnamon

1. Put the milk, cream, and cinnamon sticks into a saucepan and bring to a boil. Remove from the heat and allow to infuse for 5 minutes and then discard the cinnamon sticks.

2. Beat the egg yolks with the sugar and ground cinnamon until light and fluffy. Pour over the warm milk and cream. Stir over a gentle heat until the mixture is thick enough to coat the back of a spoon.

3. Allow to cool completely before churning in an ice-cream maker according to the manufacturer's instructions until set (thick) and then spoon into a suitable freezing container and freeze until hard (almost at once if making in a machine, but 5–6 hours if making by hand).

4. Soften at room temperature, 10–15 minutes, before serving.

STRAWBERRY & BLACK PEPPER ICE CREAM

It might seem an odd combination but a touch of black pepper really does bring out the fragrant sweetness of ripe, in-season strawberries. This is an eggless recipe and so perfect for those who prefer not to eat uncooked eggs.

SERVES 4–6

1 cup milk
1 cup whipping cream
¾ cup superfine sugar
3 cups ripe strawberries, rinsed and hulled
½ teaspoon ground black pepper

1. Put the milk, cream, and sugar in a saucepan and bring gently to boiling point. Remove from the heat and allow to cool.

2. Place the strawberries in a food processor and process until smooth. Pass through a fine sieve to remove the seeds. Stir in the black pepper, followed by the cooled milk mixture.

3. Transfer to an ice-cream maker and churn according to the manufacturer's instructions until the ice cream reaches the consistency of lightly whipped cream. Spoon into a suitable freezing container and freeze until hard (almost at once if making in a machine, but 5–6 hours if made by hand).

4. Soften at room temperature, 10–15 minutes, before serving.

CRÈME BRÛLÉE ICE CREAM

SERVES 4–6

2 fat vanilla beans
1¼ cups milk
¾ cup whipping cream
5 egg yolks
½ cup caster sugar
⅓ cup demerara sugar
Oil for greasing

1. With a sharp knife, cut down the middle of each vanilla bean lengthwise and scrape the seeds into a saucepan.

2. Add the vanilla beans and pour in the milk and cream. Slowly bring to a boil and then remove from the heat and allow to infuse for 5 minutes. Remove the beans (see tip on page 24).

3. Beat the egg yolks with the superfine sugar until light and fluffy and then pour over the vanilla milk.

4. Return to the pan, then stir over a gentle heat until the mixture is thick enough to coat the back of a spoon. Allow to cool, then churn in an ice-cream maker according to the manufacturer's instructions until set (thick).

5. Meanwhile, sprinkle the demerara sugar over the base of a skillet and leave over a gentle heat until it starts to melt and caramelize. Don't worry if it doesn't completely melt: it is good to have a few grains to crunch on.

6. Pour over an oiled baking sheet, allow to harden, and then roughly break up. Stir into the churned ice cream. Spoon the mixture into a suitable freezing container and freeze until hard (almost at once in a machine, but 5–6 hours if making by hand).

7. Soften at room temperature, 10–15 minutes, before serving.

ICE-CREAM TIP

If you have a blowtorch, you can caramelize the demerara sugar instead of heating it in a skillet. Simply sprinkle the sugar over a large lightly oiled, nonstick baking sheet. Run the blowtorch over the surface of the sugar until it starts to melt and caramelize. Allow to harden, then roughly break up and stir into the churned ice cream.

CARAMEL ICE CREAM

The trick to deep caramel-flavored ice cream is to melt the sugar until it just reaches a dark caramel color without burning. Any hint of burnt sugar will ruin the ice cream.

SERVES 4–6

1³/₄ cups milk
²/₃ cup whipping cream
¹/₂ cup superfine sugar
4 egg yolks

1. Put the milk and cream in a saucepan. Bring to a boil and then remove from the heat.

2. In a small pan, gently cook half of the superfine sugar until it melts and turns a golden caramel color. Pour half the hot milk and cream over the caramel (be careful it might splutter up) and stir over a gentle heat until the sugar melts back into the liquid. Add the remaining milk and cream, then set aside.

3. Beat the egg yolks with the remaining sugar until light and fluffy and then pour over the warm caramel. Stir over a gentle heat until the mixture is just thick enough to coat the back of a spoon.

4. Cool completely before churning in an ice-cream maker according to the manufacturer's instructions until set (thick). Spoon into a suitable freezing container and freeze until hard (almost at once if making in a machine, but 5–6 hours if making by hand).

5. Soften at room temperature, 10–15 minutes, before serving.

CHERRY & ALMOND ICE CREAM

You can serve this ice cream with a handful of toasted slivered almonds, some grated semisweet chocolate sprinkled over the top, or even some fresh cherries.

SERVES 4–6

1 cup ground almonds
1½ cups milk
¾ cup whipping cream
4 egg yolks
½ cup superfine sugar
2 teaspoons vanilla extract
1½ cups ripe cherries, pitted
   and finely chopped

1. Put the ground almonds in a large saucepan and then pour over the milk and whipping cream. Stir well and bring to a boil over a gentle heat. Remove and allow to infuse for 10 minutes.

2. Beat the egg yolks and sugar together with the vanilla extract until light and fluffy. Strain the almond milk through a fine sieve and beat into the egg yolks. Pour back into a clean pan and stir over a gentle heat until the mixture is thick enough to coat the back of a spoon.

3. Allow to cool before stirring in the chopped cherries. Churn in an ice-cream maker according to the manufacturer's instructions until set (thick). Spoon into a suitable freezing container and freeze until hard (almost at once if making in a machine, but 5–6 hours if making by hand).

4. Soften at room temperature, 10–15 minutes, before serving.

COCONUT ICE CREAM

If you are a real coconut lover, lightly toast some shredded coconut and sprinkle over the top of the ice cream just before serving.

SERVES 4–6

2½ cups canned coconut milk
5 egg yolks
¾ cups superfine sugar
¾ cup whipping cream

1. Pour the coconut milk into a saucepan and slowly bring to a boil.

2. Meanwhile, in a bowl beat together the egg yolks and sugar. Pour over the hot milk, stir, and then strain through a sieve back into the saucepan.

3. Stir over a gentle heat until the mixture just coats the back of a wooden spoon. Pour into a heatproof bowl, allow to cool, and then cover and chill.

4. Stir the cream into the chilled custard, pour into an ice-cream maker and churn according to the manufacturer's instructions until set (thick), then spoon into a suitable freezing container and freeze until hard (almost at once if making in a machine, but 5–6 hours if making by hand).

5. Soften at room temperature, 10–15 minutes, before serving.

VANILLA RICE ICE CREAM

This is a lovely rich ice cream with an unusual texture. It's basically a creamy rice pudding that has been frozen.

SERVES 4–6

¾ cup milk
¾ cup whipping cream
4 egg yolks
2 tablespoons superfine sugar
1 teaspoon vanilla extract
FOR THE RICE
1 vanilla bean, split
¾ cup Arborio (risotto) rice
2½ cups milk
6 tablespoons superfine sugar

ICE-CREAM TIP
This ice cream does not churn well in an ice-cream maker because it is extremely thick and the paddles won't turn after a while. Because of its texture and creaminess it can just be spooned into a freezing container and frozen without being beaten.

1. To make the rice, put the vanilla bean, rice, milk, and sugar into a pan. Stir over a gentle heat until the rice swells and becomes a creamy consistency with a slight bite to it, about 30 minutes.

2. Remove from the heat and allow to cool completely. Remove the vanilla bean (see tip on page 24).

3. Bring the milk and cream for the custard to a boil in a saucepan.

4. Beat the egg yolks, sugar, and vanilla extract together until thick and pale, then pour over the hot milk and cream. Return to the pan and stir over a gentle heat until the mixture coats the back of a spoon. Allow to cool.

5. Put three-quarters of the rice into a food processor and process until smooth. Stir into the cooled custard, along with the unprocessed rice. Pour into a freezing container and freeze until hard, 5–6 hours (see tip).

6. Soften at room temperature for at least 20 minutes before serving —it is much harder than other ice creams.

WHISKEY & MARMALADE ICE CREAM

Fine-cut marmalade works best here and of course it must be a good-quality brand. The sweet, jello-like marmalades don't give enough punch. This is a great ice cream to serve with a steamed pudding, ginger cake, or gingerbread.

SERVES 4–6

1¾ cups milk
⅔ cup whipping cream
4 egg yolks
½ cup superfine sugar
3 tablespoons fine-cut marmalade
1 tablespoon whiskey

1. Heat the milk and cream in a saucepan.

2. Beat together the egg yolks and sugar until light and fluffy. Pour over the hot milk and cream, stir well, and return to the pan. Stir over a gentle heat until the mixture is thick enough to coat the back of a spoon.

3. Remove from the heat and allow to cool completely. Mix the marmalade with the whiskey and stir into the cooled custard. Churn in an ice-cream maker according to the manufacturer's instructions until set (thick), then spoon into a suitable freezing container and freeze until hard (almost at once if making in a machine, but 5–6 hours if making by hand).

4. Soften at room temperature, 10–15 minutes, before serving.

BANOFFEE ICE CREAM

This is a heavenly ice cream and you could add a sprinkling of crushed cookies on top to copy a banoffee pie. Adding lemon juice to the bananas prevents discoloration of the ice cream.

SERVES 4–6

1 x quantity Dulce de leche ice cream
  (see pages 59)
2 ripe bananas
Juice of ½ lemon

1. Remove the Dulce de leche ice cream from the freezer at least 20 minutes before mixing—it needs to be quite soft but don't let it melt completely.

2. Mash the bananas until smooth and stir in the lemon juice. Stir into the ice cream and return the container to the freezer until the ice cream has frozen hard, 5–6 hours.

3. Soften at room temperature, 10–15 minutes, before serving.

BLUEBERRY SHORTCAKE ICE CREAM

You can use any type of plain cookie to make this ice cream, but a buttery shortbread I think works best here. Serve in individual bowls with extra cookies and blueberries.

SERVES 4–6

1¼ cups water
½ cup superfine sugar
1½ cups blueberries, rinsed
3oz shortbread fingers
1¼ cups ready-made fresh custard
⅔ cup whipping cream

1. Put the water and sugar in a saucepan and stir over a medium heat until the sugar has dissolved. Boil for 5 minutes, then add the blueberries and simmer for 3 minutes. Remove from the heat and allow to cool.

2. Roughly crush the shortbread fingers.

3. When the blueberry syrup is cold, stir in the custard and whipping cream. Churn in an ice-cream maker according to the manufacturer's instructions until just set (thick), then stir in the crushed shortbread and spoon into a suitable freezing container. Freeze until hard (almost at once if making by machine, but 5–6 hours if making by hand).

4. Soften at room temperature, 10–15 minutes, before serving.

RUM & RAISIN ICE CREAM

Use the plumpest, juiciest raisins you can find and leave to macerate for as long as possible in the rum.

SERVES 4

½ cup raisins, rinsed and drained
4 tablespoons dark rum
1 cup milk
¾ cup whipping cream
3 egg yolks
⅓ cup superfine sugar

1. Soak the raisins in the rum for at least 2 hours.

2. Heat the milk and cream in a saucepan. Beat the egg yolks with the sugar until light and fluffy, then pour over the hot milk.

3. Return to the pan and stir over a gentle heat until the mixture coats the back of a spoon. Allow to cool completely, then churn in an ice-cream maker according to the manufacturer's instructions until set (thick).

4. When the ice cream just holds its shape, use a spatula to scrape it into a freezing container and stir in the soaked raisins. Freeze until hard (almost at once if making in a machine, but 5–6 hours if making by hand).

5. Soften at room temperature, 10–15 minutes, before serving.

ICE-CREAM TIP
If you are short of time, gently heat up the rum in a saucepan and stir in the raisins. They will plump up more quickly, but let them cool down before stirring into the ice cream.

NOUGAT ICE CREAM

I like to use a Spanish turron in this recipe as it has a wonderful fudge-like consistency that melts into the custard. You can find it in come supermarkets, but ordinary nougat also works well.

SERVES 4–6

1³/₄ cups milk
²/₃ cup cream
3 egg yolks
¹/₂ cup superfine sugar
28oz Spanish turron or nougat

1. Bring the milk and cream to a boil in a saucepan.

2. Beat the egg yolks and sugar until light and fluffy, then pour over the hot milk and cream. Return to the pan and stir over a gentle heat until the mixture is thick enough to coat the back of a spoon. Remove from the heat and cool completely.

3. Meanwhile, finely chop the turron or nougat and then stir into the custard. Churn in an ice-cream maker according to the manufacturer's instructions until set (thick). Spoon into a suitable freezing container and freeze until hard (almost at once if making in a machine, but 5–6 hours if making by hand), if not serving at once.

4. Soften at room temperature, 10–15 minutes, before serving.

MILKY WAY ICE CREAM

Very quick and easy to make, this ice cream, made with Milky Way candy,

bars is also a really light and creamy chocolate treat.

SERVES 4

5 Milky Way bars (1½oz each),
    chopped
¾ cup milk
1¾ cups whipping cream

1. Put the chopped Milky Ways in a saucepan with the milk. Stir over a gentle heat until the confectionery has melted. Remove from the heat and allow to cool and then stir in the cream.

2. Churn in an ice-cream maker according to the manufacturer's instructions until set (thick) and then spoon into a suitable freezing container and freeze until hard (almost at once if making in a machine, but 5–6 hours if making by hand).

3. Soften at room temperature, 10–15 minutes, before serving.

ICE-CREAM TIP
*Buy an extra Milky Way bar, chop
it up, and serve the ice cream
in scoops, topped with toasted,
chopped hazelnuts and
bits of candy bar.*

LEMON CURD ICE CREAM

This is a lovely creamy ice with a smooth, lemony flavor. Delicious served as a filling for a pavlova or individual meringues or in individual bowls topped with fresh red currants.

SERVES 4

1¼ cups milk
3 egg yolks
¼ cup superfine sugar
⅔ cup crème fraîche
5 tablespoons good-quality lemon
   curd, preferably organic

1. Pour the milk into a saucepan and bring to a boil.

2. Beat the egg yolks with the superfine sugar until light and fluffy and then pour over the hot milk. Return to the pan and stir over a gentle heat until the mixture coats the back of a spoon. Remove from the heat and allow to cool completely.

3. Beat in the crème fraîche and lemon curd, then churn in an ice-cream maker according to the manufacturer's instructions until set (thick). Spoon into a suitable freezing container and freeze until hard (almost at once if making in a machine, but 5–6 hours if making by hand).

4. Soften at room temperature, 10–15 minutes, before serving.

BROWN BREAD ICE CREAM

A Seventies stalwart, this ice cream continues to be a favorite and with good reason—it has a lovely caramel flavor from the brown sugar and the brown bread adds a certain nuttiness.

SERVES 4–6

4oz brown bread, crusts removed
½ cup dark brown sugar
2 cups ready-made fresh custard
1 cup whipping cream
1 teaspoon vanilla extract

1. Preheat the oven to 350°F. Put the bread in a food processor and process to fine bread crumbs. Spread out on a baking sheet and bake in the oven for 8–10 minutes until golden.

2. Sprinkle with the sugar and return the baking sheet to the oven for an additional 8–10 minutes until the sugar starts to melt and caramelize (don't worry if some lumps remain). Cool completely.

3. Pour the custard into a bowl and stir in the cream and vanilla extract. Churn in an ice-cream maker according to the manufacturer's instructions until just starting to freeze, then stir in the caramelized bread crumbs. Spoon into a suitable freezing container and freeze until hard (almost at once if making in a machine, but 5–6 hours if making by hand).

4. Soften at room temperature, 10–15 minutes, before serving.

DULCE DE LECHE ICE CREAM

I like to swirl the caramelized condensed milk (Dulce de leche) into the custard to produce a rippled effect, but you can also beat it in. Delicious served in a cone.

SERVES 4–6

14oz can sweet condensed milk
1¾ cups milk
¾ cup whipping cream
3 egg yolks
½ cup superfine sugar
2 teaspoons vanilla extract

1. Half-fill a saucepan with water and boil the unopened can of condensed milk for 2 hours (you may need to top up the water halfway through cooking). Remove and allow to cool completely.

2. Put the milk and cream in a saucepan and bring to a boil.

3. Beat the egg yolks with the sugar and vanilla extract until light and fluffy. Pour over the hot milk and cream, return to the pan, and stir over a gentle heat until the mixture is thick enough to coat the back of a spoon. Remove from the heat and allow to cool completely.

4. Once the custard is cold, churn in an ice-cream maker according to the manufacturer's instructions until the ice cream holds its shape.

5. Working quickly so the ice cream doesn't melt, stir in the caramelized condensed milk. Spoon into a freezing container and freeze until hard (almost at once if making in a machine, but 5–6 hours if making by hand).

6. Soften at room temperature, 10–15 minutes, before serving.

CHESTNUT & MARRONS GLACÉS ICE CREAM

For the best flavor by far, use cans of French sweetened chestnut puree.

Marrons glacés (candied chestnuts) are available the gourmet sections

of supermarkets.

SERVES 4–6

1¼ cups milk
1 cup whipping cream
4 egg yolks
¼ cup superfine sugar
2 cups sweetened chestnut puree
4 marrons glacés, roughly chopped

1. Pour the milk and cream into a saucepan and bring to a boil.

2. Beat the egg yolks and sugar together until light and fluffy, then pour over the hot milk. Return to the pan and stir over a gentle heat until the mixture is thick enough to coat the back of a spoon. Remove from the heat and allow to cool completely.

3. Stir in the chestnut puree and churn in an ice-cream maker according to the manufacturer's instructions until just set (thick). Stir in the chopped marrons glacés, spoon into a suitable freezing container, and freeze until hard (almost at once if making in a machine, but 5–6 hours if making by hand).

4. Soften at room temperature, 10–15 minutes, before serving.

HONEY ICE CREAM

Look for a really delicious strong-tasting honey—anything mass-produced will taste dull in comparison. Your local farmers market or health food store should have a good selection.

SERVES 4–6

1¾ cups whipping cream
¾ cup milk
5 egg yolks
¾ cup honey

1. Put the cream and milk in a saucepan, then bring to a boil.

2. Beat the egg yolks until pale and pour over the hot cream and milk. Return to the pan and stir over a gentle heat until the mixture coats the back of a spoon. Remove from the heat and stir in the honey.

3. Allow to cool completely and then churn in an ice-cream maker according to the manufacturer's instructions until set (thick), then spoon into a suitable freezing container and freeze until hard (almost at once if making in a machine, but 5–6 hours if making by hand).

4. Soften at room temperature, 10–15 minutes, before serving.

ICE-CREAM TIP
For extra honey flavor and to add texture, stir about ¼ cup spiced honey cake crumbs or finely chopped pieces of honeycomb into the semi-frozen custard mixture.

PISTACHIO ICE CREAM

Make sure you start this ice cream a day before as the milk needs time to infuse. If you want to go for the store-bought look, add a few drops of green food coloring. Serve with extra whole and crushed pistachios

SERVES 4

1 cup shelled natural pistachios
¾ cup superfine sugar
1½ cups milk
⅔ cup whipping cream
5 egg yolks
4–5 drops of green food coloring
   (optional)

1. Preheat the oven to 350°F. Put the pistachios into a roasting pan and roast in the oven for 5–10 minutes until just golden.

2. Allow the pistachios to cool and then place in a food processor with the sugar. Process until the mixture resembles very fine bread crumbs. Transfer to a bowl.

3. Heat the milk and cream to boiling point in a saucepan, then pour over the ground pistachio mixture, stir and allow to cool. Cover and refrigerate overnight.

4. The next day, heat up the pistachio cream just to boiling point. Pour over the egg yolks, mix, and return to the pan. Stir over a gentle heat until the mixture is thick enough to coat the back of a spoon. If using green food coloring, stir in at this stage.

5. Chill, then churn in an ice-cream maker according to the manufacturer's instructions until set (thick). Spoon into a suitable freezing container and freeze until hard (almost at once if making in a machine, but 5–6 hours if making by hand).

6. Soften at room temperature, 10–15 minutes, before serving.

BLACKBERRY ICE CREAM

Making this ice cream with an egg-based custard would take away from the wonderful fresh hedgerow flavor of the blackberries, so only whipped cream is used. It is delicious served with fresh blackberries.

SERVES 4–6

3 cups blackberries, rinsed
¾ cup superfine sugar
2 cups whipping cream

1. Put the blackberries in a food processor with the sugar and blend until smooth.

2. Pass the fruit through a fine sieve and press out as much juice and pulp as possible. Discard the seeds.

3. Lightly whip the cream until soft peaks form, then fold into the blackberry puree.

4. Churn in an ice-cream maker according to the manufacturer's instructions until the ice cream just holds its shape, then spoon into a suitable freezing container and freeze until hard (almost at once if making in a machine, but 5–6 hours if making by hand).

5. Soften at room temperature, 10–15 minutes, before serving.

ICE-CREAM TIP
It is worth investing in a fine-mesh sieve, as well as a regular sieve as this will ensure no seeds escape into the ice cream. They are a little bit more expensive but a good piece of equipment for your kitchen nevertheless.

DAMSON & SLOE GIN ICE CREAM

You can find sloe gin on some supermarket shelves these days but a homemade batch will taste even better.

SERVES 4–6

10 damson plums (about 1lb), rinsed
1⅓ cups superfine sugar
4 tablespoons water
1¼ cups milk
1¼ cups whipping cream
4 egg yolks
5 tablespoons sloe gin

1. Put the damsons into a saucepan with ¾ cup of the superfine sugar and the water. Simmer over a very low heat until the damsons are soft.

2. Pass the fruit through a sieve to extract the pits and skins.

3. Pour the milk and whipping cream into a saucepan and bring to a boil.

4. Put the egg yolks into a bowl with the remaining superfine sugar. Beat until pale and thick. Pour over the hot milk and cream, and mix well.

5. Return the mixture to the pan and cook, stirring, over a low heat until thick enough to coat the back of a spoon. Remove from the heat and allow to cool completely, then stir in the damson puree and sloe gin.

6. Churn in an ice-cream maker according to the manufacturer's instructions until set (thick) and then spoon into a suitable freezing container and freeze until hard (almost at once if making in a machine, but 5–6 hours if making by hand).

7. Soften at room temperature, 10–15 minutes, before serving.

ORANGE ICE CREAM

Boiling the orange juice really intensifies the flavor
of this ice and the zest prevents it from being too sickly sweet.

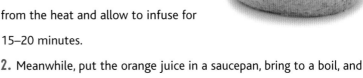

SERVES 5–6

Grated zest and juice of 4 rinsed
    oranges
1 cup milk
1¹⁄₂ cups whipping cream
5 egg yolks
²⁄₃ cup superfine sugar

1. Put the orange zest in a saucepan
with the milk and cream. Slowly
bring to a boil and then remove
from the heat and allow to infuse for
15–20 minutes.

2. Meanwhile, put the orange juice in a saucepan, bring to a boil, and
bubble until reduced by half, about 10 minutes.

3. Beat the egg yolks and sugar until pale and frothy, then pour over the
infused milk. Return to the pan and cook over a gentle heat, stirring, until
the mixture coats the back of a spoon.

4. Remove from the heat and stir in the reduced orange juice. Cool and
churn in an ice-cream maker according to the manufacturer's
instructions until set (thick) and then spoon into a suitable freezing
container and freeze until hard (almost at once if making in a
machine, but 5–6 hours if making by hand).

5. Soften at room temperature, 10–15 minutes, before serving.

ICE-CREAM TIP
*This ice cream looks pretty in
hollowed-out oranges. Slice the tops
from 5–6 oranges and remove a little
slice from each base so the oranges stand
up. Scoop out the flesh and pith, then
fill with slightly softened orange ice
cream. Return to the freezer until
the ice cream is hard,
1–2 hours.*

PRUNE & ARMAGNAC ICE CREAM

Use plump, ready-to-eat pitted prunes for this ice cream. If you don't have Armagnac in your drinks cabinet you can use cognac instead.

SERVES 4

³/₄ cup pitted prunes, finely chopped
4 tablespoons Armagnac
1³/₄ cups milk
²/₃ cup whipping cream
4 egg yolks
¹/₂ cup superfine sugar

1. Soak the chopped prunes in the Armagnac for at least 30 minutes, preferably 2–3 hours.

2. Heat the milk and cream in a saucepan. Beat together the egg yolks and superfine sugar until light and fluffy. Pour over the hot milk and cream, stir well and then return to the pan. Stir over a gentle heat until the mixture is thick enough to coat the back of a spoon. Remove from the heat and allow to cool completely.

3. When cold stir in the prunes and Armagnac. Churn in an ice-cream maker according to the manufacturer's instructions until set (thick).

4. Serve immediately or freeze until hard in a freezing container (almost at once if making in a machine, but 5–6 hours if making by hand).

5. Soften at room temperature, 10–15 minutes, before serving.

QUICK APPLE ICE CREAM

This is a great standby pantry ice cream; young children seem to enjoy its mild, creamy flavor.

SERVES 4–6

¼ cup superfine sugar
1¼ cups ready-made custard
⅔ cup whipping cream
FOR THE COMPÔTE
1¼lb dessert apples, peeled, cored, and cut into small chunks
6 tablespoons water
1–2 tablespoons superfine sugar

1. First, make the compôte. Put the apples and water into a saucepan and cook over a gentle heat until the apples are soft, about 10–15 minutes.

2. Cool before transferring to a food processor and blend until smooth. Taste and add the sugar if the compôte is a little tart.

3. Mix all the ingredients, including the compôte, together in a bowl.

4. Transfer to an ice-cream maker and churn according to the manufacturer's instructions until set (thick). Spoon into a suitable freezing container and freeze until hard (almost at once if making in a machine, but 5–6 hours if making by hand).

5. Soften at room temperature, 10–15 minutes, before serving.

ICE-CREAM TIP
For a spiced version, add a pinch of cinnamon and a pinch of ground cloves to the apple compôte.

STEM GINGER ICE CREAM

The gingerroot gives a fresh, zingy flavor to this ice cream while the stem ginger, which is milder in flavor, adds a bit of texture.

SERVES 4–6

1 thumb-size piece of fresh
    gingerroot, peeled and sliced
1¼ cups milk
¾ cup whipping cream
5 egg yolks
½ cup superfine sugar
4 knobs of stem ginger in syrup,
    finely chopped

1. Put the sliced ginger in a saucepan with the milk and cream. Slowly bring to a boil and allow to infuse for 5 minutes. Pass through a sieve and discard the ginger.

2. Beat the egg yolks with the superfine sugar until light and fluffy. Pour over the ginger-infused milk.

3. Return to the pan and stir over a gentle heat until the mixture is thick enough to coat the back of a spoon. Remove from the heat and allow to cool.

4. Churn the cold custard in an ice-cream maker according to the manufacturer's instructions until just set (thick), then stir in the chopped stem ginger and spoon into a suitable freezing container. Freeze until hard (almost at once if making in a machine, but 5–6 hours if making by hand).

5. Soften at room temperature, 10–15 minutes, before serving.

FESTIVE ICE CREAM

For those people who don't particularly enjoy the heaviness of a Christmas pudding but still like the taste of dried and candied fruits and nuts.

SERVES 6

¼ cup mixed candied fruit, such as candied peel and candied cherries
½ cup golden raisins
2 tablespoons currants
2 tablespoons brandy
3 tablespoons finely chopped almonds
1¼ cups milk
1 cup whipping cream
3 egg yolks
6 tablespoons superfine sugar

1. Put the candied fruit, golden raisins, currants, and brandy in a bowl and allow to macerate for 2–3 hours. Stir in the almonds.

2. Heat the milk and cream to boiling point in a saucepan. Beat the egg yolks with the superfine sugar until light and fluffy, then pour over the milk and cream.

3. Stir well, then return to the pan and stir over a low heat until the mixture is thick enough to coat the back of a spoon. Allow to cool completely.

4. Churn in an ice-cream maker according to the manufacturer's instructions until just on the point of setting, then spoon into a bowl and quickly stir in the macerated fruit and nuts. Spoon into a suitable freezing container and freeze until hard (almost at once if making in a machine, but 5–6 hours if making by hand).

5. Soften at room temperature, 10–15 minutes, before serving.

LAVENDER ICE CREAM

Quite possibly one of my favorite ice creams—served with a slice of buttery shortbread, this is one of the best desserts you could offer up.

SERVES 4—6

2 cups milk
1¼ cups whipping cream
2 tablespoons lavender flower heads
4 egg yolks
½ cup superfine sugar

1. Put the milk, cream, and lavender heads in a saucepan and bring to a boil. Remove from the heat and infuse for 5 minutes, then pass through a sieve.

2. Beat the egg yolks and superfine sugar together until light and fluffy, then pour over the infused milk and cream.

3. Stir over a gentle heat until the mixture is thick enough to coat the back of a spoon. Remove from the heat and allow to cool completely.

4. Churn in an ice-cream maker according to the manufacturer's instructions until set (thick) and then spoon into a suitable freezing container and freeze until hard (almost at once if making in a machine, but 5–6 hours if making by hand).

5. Soften at room temperature, 10–15 minutes, before serving.

ICE-CREAM TIP
At the end of the summer, dry the heads from your lavender bushes and keep them in an airtight container to use all year round. Dried lavender is more potent, however, so you will only need a tablespoon of dried heads to infuse the milk.

MARSHMALLOW & MACADAMIA ICE CREAM

Macadamia nuts are expensive but have a unique mild, buttery flavor that works wonderfully well with an ice cream. Use a bigger saucepan than you would normally use—the marshmallows take up a lot of room before melting into the custard.

SERVES 4–6

1½ cups milk
1 cup whipping cream
2 cups marshmallows
4 egg yolks
¼ cup superfine sugar
½ cup macadamia nuts, lightly
   toasted and roughly chopped

1. Put the milk, cream, and marshmallows in a large pan. Bring to just under boiling point, then remove from the heat and stir until the marshmallows have melted.

2. Beat the egg yolks and superfine sugar until light and fluffy. Pour over the hot marshmallow milk, return to the pan, and stir over a gentle heat until the mixture is thick enough to coat the back of a spoon. Remove from the heat and allow to cool completely.

3. Churn in an ice-cream maker according to the manufacturer's instructions until just set (thick), then stir in the macadamia nuts. Spoon into a suitable freezing container and freeze until hard (almost at once if making in a machine, but 5–6 hours if making by hand).

4. Soften at room temperature, 10–15 minutes, before serving.

PECAN & MAPLE SYRUP ICE CREAM

If you can't find pecans you could use walnuts, but they don't have quite the same buttery mellowness of a pecan nut. Only real maple syrup will do— maple-flavored syrup is much sweeter and more synthetic tasting. Serve topped with extra syrup and pecans—delicious.

SERVES 4–6

¾ cup shelled pecan nuts
1¾ cups milk
⅔ cup whipping cream
3 egg yolks
6 tablespoons superfine sugar
5 tablespoons maple syrup

1. Lightly toast the pecans in a hot skillet for 3–4 minutes. Allow to cool, then roughly chop and set aside.

2. Put the milk and cream in a saucepan and bring to a boil.

3. Beat the egg yolks and sugar until light and fluffy, then pour over the hot milk and cream. Return to the pan and stir over a gentle heat until the mixture is thick enough to coat the back of a spoon. Remove from the heat and cool completely.

4. Stir in the maple syrup and cooled, chopped pecans and churn in an ice-cream maker according to the manufacturer's instructions until set (thick), then spoon into a suitable freezing container, or individual molds, if preferred, and freeze until hard (almost at once if making in a machine, but 5–6 hours if making by hand).

5. Soften at room temperature, 10–15 minutes, before serving.

GREEN TEA ICE CREAM

Try and find a really good-quality green tea, preferably organic, for this recipe—
you will notice the difference in taste. I use a powdered green tea from Japan,
which gives the ice cream a wonderful color, but ordinary green tea bags will do.

SERVES 4–6

¾ superfine sugar
2 cups water
Juice of 1 lemon
3 green tea bags
1¼ cups whipping cream

1. Put the sugar, water, and lemon juice into a saucepan and bring to the boil, stirring, to dissolve the sugar.

2. Add the tea bags, then remove from the heat and allow to infuse for at least 30 minutes. Remove the tea bags and cool completely.

3. Pour the tea syrup into an ice-cream maker and churn according to the manufacturer's instructions until just starting to freeze and thicken. Pour in the cream and continue to churn until set (thick), then spoon into a suitable freezing container and freeze until hard (almost at once if making in a machine, but 5–6 hours if making by hand).

4. Soften at room temperature, 10–15 minutes, before serving.

ROQUEFORT ICE CREAM

I like to serve a teaspoon of this ice cream in a hot soup, or on top of a plain cheddar cheese soufflé. Use homemade mayonnaise or a good-quality store-bought one, but never salad cream!

MAKES JUST UNDER 2 CUPS

4oz Roquefort cheese, crumbled
2 heaping tablespoons mayonnaise
5 heaping tablespoons crème fraîche
A little ground black pepper

1. Mash the crumbled Roquefort with a fork until smooth and then beat in the mayonnaise.

2. Stir in the crème fraîche and season with a little ground black pepper (you won't need salt because the cheese is naturally very salty).

3. Churn in an ice-cream maker according to the manufacturer's instructions for 10–15 minutes until the ice cream is just about to harden. Scrape into a small freezing container and freeze hard, about 1 hour, if not using straightaway.

4. Soften at room temperature, 10–15 minutes, before serving.

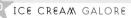

WASABI ICE CREAM

This ice is not served alone but as a condiment to fish and meat dishes. It is especially good with sushi or a slice or two of rare beef tenderloin.

MAKES JUST UNDER 2 CUPS

1¼ cups crème fraîche
Juice of ½ lemon
3 teaspoons wasabi paste (see tip)
Ground sea salt, to taste

1. Mix together the crème fraîche, lemon juice, and wasabi paste until smooth, then taste and season with salt.

2. Churn in an ice-cream maker according to the manufacturer's instructions until stiff, then scoop into a suitable freezing container and freeze until hard (almost at once if making in a machine, but 5–6 hours if making by hand).

3. Soften at room temperature, 10–15 minutes, before serving.

ICE-CREAM TIP

Wasabi is a Japanese horseradish that they serve with sushi. It is bright green and normally sold in tubes. Once opened, store in the refrigerator, where it will keep fresh for months. Wasabi is occasionally sold in powdered form— in which case, mix it with a little water as you would for powdered mustard.

HORSERADISH ICE CREAM

This is delicious served as a spoonful dropped into a warm tomato soup, or on the side with some smoked salmon or smoked eel.

MAKES JUST UNDER 2 CUPS

¾ cup cream cheese
⅔ cup crème fraîche
4 teaspoons horseradish sauce
Pinch of salt and ground white
   pepper

1. In a bowl, mix together the cream cheese, crème fraîche, and horseradish sauce. Taste, then season with a little salt and ground white pepper.

2. Churn in an ice-cream maker according to the manufacturer's instructions for about 10 minutes until the mixture is thick, but not too frozen. Scoop into a small freezing container and freeze until hard (about 1 hour if making in a machine, but overnight if making by hand).

3. Soften at room temperature for at least 20 minutes before serving—it is much harder than other ice creams.

ICE-CREAM TIP
Remember that the freezing process dulls sweet and savory flavors so you need to be a bit bolder and slightly overseason with salt and pepper before freezing this ice cream.

TOMATO ICE CREAM

The key, as always, to a good fruit ice cream is the quality and ripeness of the fruit itself. Try to find some good vine-ripened tomatoes, or better still, home grown.

MAKES JUST OVER 2 CUPS

1 tablespoon olive oil
1 onion, finely chopped
1lb ripe, flavorsome tomatoes, quartered
2 garlic cloves, finely chopped
1 bay leaf
2 teaspoons superfine sugar
1¼ cups whipping cream
Salt and ground black pepper

1. Put the olive oil in a saucepan and warm through. Add the chopped onion and cook over a low heat for 10 minutes until the onions are softened.

2. Add the tomatoes, garlic cloves, bay leaf, sugar, and a grind or two of salt and ground black pepper. Cook over a low heat for at least 20 minutes until the tomatoes have softened to a pulp.

3. Remove from the heat and allow to cool a little before pressing through a sieve. Discard the seeds and skins.

4. Cool completely before stirring in the cream. Taste and check the seasoning.

5. Churn in an ice-cream maker according to the manufacturer's instructions until set (thick), then spoon into a suitable freezing container and freeze until hard (almost at once if making in a machine, but 5–6 hours if making by hand).

6. Soften at room temperature, 10–15 minutes, before serving.

ICE-CREAM TIP
If you cannot find ripe, flavorsome tomatoes add a tablespoon of tomato paste when you add the tomato to the softened onions.

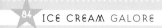
RATATOUILLE ICE CREAM

Remember when seasoning this ice cream that it loses flavor when frozen, so be bold with the salt and pepper. Serve in small glasses as an appetizer and garnish with fresh marjoram leaves.

SERVES 4–6

2 cups good store-bought ratatouille
(from health food shops)
1 cup plain yogurt
²/₃ cup whipping cream,
lightly whipped
Salt and ground black pepper

1. Put the ratatouille in a food processor and process until smooth.

2. Pass through a fine sieve and stir in the plain yogurt and whipped cream. Taste, then season with salt and ground black pepper.

3. Churn in an ice-cream maker according to the manufacturer's instructions until set (thick), then spoon into a suitable freezing container and freeze until hard (about 1 hour if making in a machine, but overnight if making by hand).

4. Soften at room temperature, 10–15 minutes, before serving.

FETA CHEESE & BLACK OLIVE RIPPLE ICE CREAM

I have served this ice cream to accompany broiled salmon fillets and it works wonderfully well. Put a spoonful on top of the warm salmon and allow it to melt and become a delicious sauce.

MAKES JUST UNDER 3 CUPS

4oz feta cheese
1 cup crème fraîche
1¼ cups whipping cream
3 teaspoons tapenade (black olive paste)
Salt and ground white pepper

1. Put the feta, crème fraîche, and whipping cream in a food processor and process until smooth. Taste, then season with a little salt and ground white pepper.

2. Pour into an ice-cream maker and churn according to the manufacturer's instructions until just on the point of freezing.

3. Spoon into a freezing container, then add the tapenade and swirl through the cream for a rippled effect. Freeze until hard, about 1–2 hours.

4. Soften at room temperature, 10–15 minutes, before serving.

GOAT CHEESE & BASIL ICE CREAM

Being a very thick base mixture, this ice cream doesn't churn well in an ice-cream maker but it can be spooned into a freezing container and frozen immediately. I like to serve it in spoonfuls on top of a spicy tomato tart.

MAKES JUST UNDER 2 CUPS

10oz goat cheese
½ cup crème fraîche
4 tablespoons mayonnaise
1 tablespoon finely chopped basil

1. Mix together the goat cheese, crème fraîche, mayonnaise, and chopped basil until smooth.

2. Spoon into a freezing container and freeze until hard, about 1 hour.

3. Soften at room temperature for at least 20 minutes before serving—it is much harder than other ice creams.

ICE-CREAM TIP
Fresh goat cheese is mild in flavor with a lovely light, slightly whipped texture. It is normally sold in little pyramid-shaped cartons. Don't try and make this ice cream with the harder, log-shaped goat cheese—the texture would be too grainy.

FROSTED DELIGHTS

APPLE & CALVADOS SORBET

Calvados is an apple brandy that is made in the north of France. If you can't find Calvados, there are many fine apple brandies now produced.

SERVES 4

4 sweet dessert apples, peeled,
    cored, and roughly chopped
²/₃ cup superfine sugar
2¹/₂ cups water
Juice of 1 lemon
3 tablespoons Calvados
1 egg white, lightly beaten

1. Place the apples in a saucepan with the sugar and water. Bring to a boil and then turn the heat down and simmer until the apples are really soft, about 20 minutes.

2. Cool a little, then pour into the food processor with the lemon juice and Calvados. Process until smooth and then chill until completely cold.

3. Churn in an ice-cream maker according to the manufacturer's instructions until just beginning to set, then pour in the beaten egg white and continue to churn until set (thick). If not serving straightaway, spoon into a suitable freezing container and freeze until hard (almost at once if making in a machine, but 5–6 hours if making by hand).

4. Soften at room temperature, 5–10 minutes, before serving.

BLACK CURRANT & CASSIS SORBET

I think black currants are the perfect fruits for ices, whether they be ice cream or sorbets, as their intense flavor stands up to the dulling of freezing.

SERVES 4–6

1 cup superfine sugar
2½ cups water
3½ cups black currants, stalks
 removed and rinsed
5 tablespoons crème de cassis
1 egg white, lightly beaten

1. Put the sugar and water into a saucepan and stir over a medium heat until the sugar has dissolved. Simmer for 10 minutes, then add the black currants and continue cooking for an additional 5 minutes.

2. Cool a little, then strain through a sieve, squashing out as much juice from the fruit as possible. Stir in the crème de cassis. Allow to cool completely, then chill for 30 minutes.

3. Churn in an ice-cream maker according to the manufacturer's instructions until the sorbet just begins to hold its shape and then pour in the beaten egg white. Continue to churn until firm and then freeze until hard (almost at once if making in a machine, but 5–6 hours if making by hand).

4. Soften at room temperature, 5–10 minutes, before serving.

BLOOD ORANGE SORBET

This is a great thirst-quenching sorbet to serve on a hot day, or to refresh the palate between courses. When blood oranges are hard to find, I use ready-squeezed orange juice. Look for cartons of blood orange juice (sometimes called Sanguinello) in the chiller cabinets next to the fresh juices.

SERVES 4

3 cups blood orange juice
⅓ cup superfine sugar

1. Mix the orange juice with the sugar and stir until the sugar has dissolved. Chill for 30 minutes.

2. Churn in an ice-cream maker according to the manufacturer's instructions until set (thick). If not serving straightaway, spoon into a suitable freezing container and freeze until hard (almost at once if making in a machine, but 5–6 hours if making by hand).

3. Soften at room temperature, 5–10 minutes, before serving.

ICE-CREAM TIP
This sorbet looks and tastes wonderful accompanied by a citrus fruit salad of segments of ruby grapefruit, plain grapefruit, and oranges. Decorate with a few mint leaves.

ELDERFLOWER SORBET

There are a lot of really good natural elderflower cordials on the market these days. Look in your local health food store, as it should have a good selection of organic ones to try.

SERVES 4

2½ cups water
1 cup superfine sugar
3 tablespoons elderflower cordial
Juice of 2 lemons

1. Put the water and sugar together in a pan and stir over a medium heat until the sugar has dissolved. Simmer for 10 minutes and then remove from the heat and allow to cool.

2. Stir in the elderflower cordial and the lemon juice. Chill for 30 minutes and then churn in an ice-cream maker according to the manufacturer's instructions until set (thick).

3. If not serving straightaway, spoon into a suitable freezing container and freeze until hard (almost at once if making in a machine, or 5–6 hours if making by hand).

4. Soften at room temperature, 5–10 minutes, before serving.

CHOCOLATE SORBET

This sorbet is deliciously rich, but as it has no eggs or cream it is sharper and cleaner tasting than a chocolate ice cream.

SERVES 4

1 cup superfine sugar
$\frac{1}{2}$ cup cocoa powder
2oz plain chocolate
   (50% cocoa solids)
2$\frac{1}{2}$ cups water

1. Place all the ingredients in a saucepan and heat slowly, stirring until smooth. Bring to a boil and simmer for 5 minutes, then remove from the heat and allow to cool completely.

2. Churn in an ice-cream maker according to the manufacturer's instructions until set (thick). If not serving straightaway, spoon into a suitable freezing container and freeze until hard (almost at once if making in a machine, but 5–6 hours if making by hand).

3. Soften at room temperature, 5–10 minutes, before serving.

PEACH & RASPBERRY SORBET

The two fruits complement each other very well. If you want to make this sorbet and ripe peaches are not in season, then canned peaches make an admirable alternative.

SERVES 4

$\frac{1}{2}$ cup superfine sugar
$1\frac{1}{4}$ cups water
4 ripe peaches, rinsed
$2\frac{1}{2}$ cups raspberries, rinsed
1 egg white, lightly beaten

1. Put the sugar and water into a saucepan and stir over a medium heat until the sugar has dissolved. Simmer for 5 minutes, then remove from the heat and cool.

2. Bring a pan of water to a boil and drop in the peaches. Leave for 10 seconds, then remove and plunge into cold water. Peel off the skins, then halve and remove the pits.

3. Transfer the peach flesh to a food processor and process until smooth. Stir into the cold sugar syrup.

4. Put the raspberries in the food processor and process for a few seconds until they have broken down. Pass through a fine sieve to remove the seeds, pressing out as much juice as possible. Stir into the peach mixture and chill for 30 minutes.

5. Churn in an ice-cream maker according to the manufacturer's instructions until just beginning to hold its shape, then pour in the beaten egg white.

6. Continue to churn until set (thick). Freeze until hard if not serving at once (almost at once in a machine, but 5–6 hours if making by hand).

BRAMBLE SORBET

Blackberries aren't reserved for crumbles! This is a delicious sorbet, especially when made with the freshly picked fall harvest of blackberries.

SERVES 4–6

1¼ cups water
⅔ cup superfine sugar
3 cups blackberries, rinsed
Juice of 1 lemon
1 egg white, lightly beaten

1. Put the water and sugar in a saucepan and stir over a medium heat until the sugar has dissolved. Boil for 5 minutes and then remove from the heat and allow to cool completely.

2. Put the blackberries in a food processor with the cooled sugar syrup and process until smooth. Pass through a fine sieve and discard the seeds.

3. Stir in the lemon juice, then churn in an ice-cream maker according to the manufacturer's instructions until just slushy.

4. Pour in the lightly beaten egg white and then continue to churn until frozen and doubled in size. If not serving straightaway, spoon into a suitable freezing container and freeze until hard (almost at once if making in a machine, but 5–6 hours if making by hand).

5. Soften at room temperature, 5–10 minutes, before serving.

ICE-CREAM TIP
As the bramble season is short, it is a good idea to freeze some just-picked fruit that you can use at a later date. There is no need to freeze blackberries individually, if using in a sorbet or sauce. Simply put in a freezer bag, label, and freeze. Defrost before using.

CLEMENTINE GRANITA

This works just as well with mandarins or indeed oranges, but for the best flavor choose clementines.

SERVES 4–6

8 clementines, rinsed
1¼ cups water
⅓ cup superfine sugar

1. Use a vegetable peeler to finely pare the zest from 4 clementines without leaving too much white pith. Place in a saucepan with the water and sugar. Bring to a boil, stirring, to dissolve the sugar.

2. Boil for 5 minutes, then remove from the heat and cool. Remove the pared zest and discard.

3. Squeeze the juice from all the clementines and pour into the cooled syrup. Stir and then chill for 30 minutes.

4. Pour into a shallow freezing container and freeze for about 1 hour, then scrape around the edges with a fork to disperse the ice crystals. Continue to scrape around the sides every 30–40 minutes for 4–5 hours until the mixture is firm, but not frozen solid.

MELON SORBET

I like to use orangey-yellow Charentais melon—I don't think you can beat their flavor when ripened by the summer sun. Don't try making this sorbet unless you are confident that the melons are really, really ripe.

SERVES 4

2 ripe Charentais or cantaloupe melons, about 3lb
Juice of 1 lemon
1/3 cup fructose
2 tablespoons eau de vie (melon liqueur) (optional)
1 egg white, lightly beaten

1. Halve the melons and scoop out the seeds. Put the flesh into a food processor with the lemon juice, fructose, and eau de vie (if using). Process until smooth, then chill for 30 minutes.

2. Churn in an ice-cream maker according to the manufacturer's instructions until set (thick), but not frozen.

3. Pour in the beaten egg white and continue to churn until frozen, then spoon into a suitable freezing container and freeze until hard if not serving straightaway (almost at once if making in a machine, but 5–6 hours if making by hand).

4. Soften at room temperature, 5–10 minutes, before serving.

ICE-CREAM TIP
Fructose is a natural sugar and brings out the flavor of the fruit especially well. However, it is still a sugar and therefore unsuitable as a substitute sweetener for diabetics or those on calorie-controlled diets. Look for eau de vie de melon in speciality liquor stores, or in supermarkets if you are in France.

PINEAPPLE SORBET

You may need to adjust the sugar in this sorbet as the sweetness in pineapple can vary greatly. If the pineapple is a little tart, add about 2 tablespoons more sugar.

SERVES 4–6

1½ cups water
⅓ superfine sugar
1½ cups cubed pineapple flesh
1 egg white, lightly beaten

1. Put the water and sugar in a saucepan and stir over a medium heat until the sugar has dissolved. Boil for 5 minutes and then remove from the heat and allow to cool completely.

2. Put the pineapple flesh in a food processor and process until smooth. Stir into the cooled sugar syrup.

3. Churn in an ice-cream maker according to the manufacturer's instructions until slushy, then pour in the beaten egg white. Continue to churn until set (thick). If not serving straightaway, spoon into a suitable freezing container and freeze until hard (almost at once if making in a machine, but 5–6 hours if making by hand).

4. Soften at room temperature, 5–10 minutes, before serving.

KIWIFRUIT SORBET

Often kiwifruit are as hard as rocks when sold in the stores so buy them ahead of time to ensure they are really sweet and ripe for the sorbet. This is a great recipe to make into popsicles.

SERVES 4–6

²/₃ cup superfine sugar
1¼ cups water
Juice of 1 lemon
5 ripe kiwifruit, rinsed
1 egg white, lightly beaten

1. Put the sugar, water, and lemon juice in a saucepan and stir over a medium heat until the sugar has dissolved. Simmer for 5 minutes, then remove from the heat and cool completely.

2. Halve the kiwifruit and scoop the flesh into a food processor. Add the cooled sugar syrup and process until smooth. Chill for 30 minutes.

3. Churn in an ice-cream maker according to the manufacturer's instructions until the sorbet just begins to hold its shape, then add the beaten egg white and churn until set (thick).

4. If not serving straightaway, spoon into a suitable freezing container and freeze until hard (almost at once if making in a machine, but 5–6 hours if making by hand).

5. Soften at room temperature, 5–10 minutes, before serving.

CUCUMBER GRANITA

This is a refreshing granita to serve pre-dessert, especially a rich dessert, as it cleanses the palate.

SERVES 4

2 cucumbers, rinsed, peeled, and
   roughly chopped
$^2/_3$ cup superfine sugar
Juice of 1 lemon

1. Put the cucumbers and sugar in a food processor and process until the mixture is smooth.

2. Pour into a fine sieve placed over a bowl and extract as much juice as possible. Discard the pulp.

3. Stir in the lemon juice, pour into a shallow freezing container, and freeze for 1 hour.

4. Scrape around the edges with a fork to disperse the ice crystals. Continue to scrape around the sides every 30–40 minutes for 4–5 hours until the mixture is firm, but not frozen solid.

5. Soften at room temperature, 5–10 minutes, before serving.

COSMOPOLITAN SORBET

Beloved cocktail of many, this translates into a wonderful sorbet. If you want to up the alcohol content, pour a single shot of ice-cold vodka over the sorbet just before serving.

SERVES 4–6

1¼ cups water
½ cup superfine sugar
2 cups cranberry juice
¾ cup grapefruit juice
3 tablespoons vodka

1. Put the water and sugar into a saucepan and stir over a medium heat until the sugar has dissolved. Boil for 5 minutes and then remove from the heat and allow to cool completely.

2. When the sugar syrup is cold, stir in the cranberry and grapefruit juices and the vodka. Chill for 30 minutes.

3. Churn in an ice-cream maker according to the manufacturer's instructions until set (thick). If not serving straightaway, spoon into a suitable freezing container and freeze until hard (almost at once if making in a machine, but 5–6 hours if making by hand).

4. Soften at room temperature, 5–10 minutes, before serving.

LEMON & LIME SORBET

This really zingy sorbet will be a favorite with everyone. Use unwaxed, untreated lemons and limes—they are better for you and have no unpleasant aftertaste.

SERVES 6

3 lemons, rinsed
2 limes, rinsed
1 cup superfine sugar
2½ cups water
1 egg white, lightly beaten

1. Pare 3 strips from each lemon and lime. Place in a saucepan with the sugar and water. Slowly bring to a boil, stirring, so the sugar dissolves and then boil for 5 minutes.

2. Remove from the heat and allow to infuse for 30 minutes, then remove the pared zest and discard.

3. Squeeze the juice from the lemons and limes and add to the cooled sugar syrup.

4. Chill for 30 minutes, then churn in an ice-cream maker according to the manufacturer's instructions until just beginning to firm up. Pour in the beaten egg white and continue to churn until set (thick). If not serving straightaway, spoon into a suitable freezing container and freeze until hard (almost at once if making in a machine, but 5–6 hours if making by hand).

5. Soften at room temperature, 5–10 minutes, before serving.

POMELO SORBET

You could substitute grapefruit for the pomelos but you may need to add a little more sugar, because pomelos tend to be slightly sweeter.

SERVES 4

1¼ cups water
½ cup superfine sugar
3 pomelos, rinsed
1 egg white, lightly beaten

1. Put the water and sugar into a saucepan. Using a vegetable peeler, pare the zest from 1 pomelo, being careful not to take too much white pith, which can be very bitter.

2. Add the pomelo zest to the saucepan and bring to a boil, stirring, to dissolve the sugar. Simmer for 10 minutes, then remove from the heat and allow to cool completely.

3. Squeeze the juice from the pomelos and stir into the sugar syrup. Chill for 1 hour.

4. Remove the pieces of pomelo zest, then churn in an ice-cream maker according to the manufacturer's instructions until just slushy.

5. Pour in the beaten egg white and continue to churn until set (thick). If not serving straightaway, spoon into a suitable freezing container and freeze until hard (almost at once if making in a machine, but 5–6 hours if making by hand).

6. Soften at room temperature, 5–10 minutes, before serving.

ELDERFLOWER & GOOSEBERRY GRANITA

Elderflower and gooseberry must be one of the best combinations around—
the two complement each other so well. Early gooseberries may be slightly
tart, so add a little more sugar.

SERVES 4–6

2 cups water, plus 2 tablespoons
1 cup superfine sugar
2 tablespoons elderflower cordial
½ cup gooseberries, rinsed and hulled

1. Put the water and three quarters of the sugar into a saucepan and stir over a medium heat until the sugar has dissolved. Boil for 5 minutes and then remove from the heat and stir in the elderflower cordial. Allow to cool completely.

2. Put the gooseberries, 2 tablespoons water, and the remaining sugar in a pan and cook over a really gentle heat until the gooseberries are soft. Pass through a sieve to remove the seeds.

3. Stir the smooth gooseberry puree into the sugar and elderflower syrup. Chill for 30 minutes.

4. Pour into a shallow freezing container and freeze for 1 hour, then scrape around the edges with a fork to disperse the ice crystals. Continue to scrape around the sides every 30–40 minutes for 4–5 hours until the mixture is firm, but not frozen solid.

5. Soften at room temperature, 5–10 minutes, before serving.

PASSION FRUIT SORBET

With its extraordinary, strong-flavored juice, passion fruit must be one of the most perfumed fruits around. Wait until the fruit is dry and wrinkled before extracting the juice and pulp.

SERVES 4

10 ripe passion fruit
1¾ cups water
1 cup superfine sugar
Juice of 1 lemon
1 egg white

ICE-CREAM TIP
If you are unable to eat egg whites this recipe also works well if they are omitted. The sorbet will be denser and and more like a water ice.

1. Slice the passion fruit in half and scoop out the pulp and seeds into a sieve resting over a bowl. Extract as much juice as possible from the seeds and pulp.

2. Put the water and sugar in a saucepan and stir over a medium heat until the sugar has dissolved. Boil for 5 minutes and then remove from the heat and allow to cool completely.

3. Once the syrup is cold, stir in the passion fruit juice and lemon juice, then lightly beat the egg white and gently fold it through the mixture.

4. Churn in an ice-cream maker according to the manufacturer's instructions until set (thick). If not serving straightaway, spoon into a suitable freezing container and freeze until hard (almost at once if making in a machine, but 5–6 hours if making by hand).

5. Soften at room temperature, 5–10 minutes, before serving.

QUINCE SORBET

Uncooked quinces are inedible but they take on a new form when cooked in sugar syrup. Add a touch of cinnamon and star anise for a change of flavor.

SERVES 4–6

4 quinces, about 1lb, fine down brushed off, peeled, and cut into quarters, cores removed
4 cups water
1 cup superfine sugar
Juice of 1 lemon

1. Put the quinces in a saucepan with the water and sugar. Stir over a gentle heat until the sugar has dissolved. Cover and cook for about 1¼ hours until the fruit is soft. Remove from the heat and allow to cool completely.

2. Lift out the quinces and transfer to a food processor. Measure out ³⁄₄ cup of the cooking syrup and add to the food processor with the lemon juice. Process until smooth, then chill for 30 minutes.

3. Churn in an ice-cream maker according to the manufacturer's instructions until set (thick). If not serving straightaway, spoon into a suitable freezing container and freeze until hard (almost at once if making in a machine, but 5–6 hours if making by hand).

4. Soften at room temperature, 5–10 minutes, before serving.

STRAWBERRY SPOOM

A spoom is a light, frothy sorbet, that is a sorbet base with an uncooked meringue base added to it, but it is not churned in the usual manner. The name is supposedly derived from the Italian *spumante* meaning frothy or fizzy.

SERVES 4–6

1¼ cups water
½ cup superfine sugar
1⅔ cups ripe strawberries, rinsed
   and hulled
2 egg whites
⅓ cups granulated sugar

1. Put the water and sugar in a saucepan and stir over a medium heat until the sugar has dissolved, then bring to a boil for 5 minutes. Remove from the heat and allow to cool completely.

2. Once cold, pour into a food processor and add the strawberries. Process until smooth, then chill for 30 minutes.

3. Beat the egg whites to soft peaks, then beat in the granulated sugar, 1 tablespoon at a time. Fold into the chilled strawberry puree, spoon into a suitable freezing container and freeze until almost hard, about 2–3 hours.

4. Soften at room temperature, 5–10 minutes, before serving.

CAMPARI & ORANGE GRANITA

Campari and orange is a match made in heaven. Wonderful served at a cocktail party.

SERVES 4–6

1³/₄ cups water
¹/₃ cup superfine sugar
Juice of 2 oranges
5 tablespoons Campari

1. Put the water and sugar in a pan and stir over a gentle heat until the sugar has dissolved, then boil for 5 minutes. Remove from the heat and allow to cool completely.

2. Stir in the orange juice and Campari, then pour into a shallow freezing container and freeze for 1 hour.

3. Scrape around the edges of the granita with a fork to disperse the ice crystals. Continue to scrape around the sides every 30–40 minutes for 4–5 hours, until the mixture is firm, but not frozen solid.

4. Soften at room temperature, 5–10 minutes, before serving.

RUM PUNCH SORBET

This sorbet has all the flavors of the Caribbean. If you can, use dark rum—
it has a better flavor than the clear varieties. Angostura bitters are used to
colour Pink Gin and, as the name suggests, they add a subtle, but bitter
aromatic flavor to this exotic sorbet.

SERVES 4–6

1 cup water
¼ cup light brown sugar
2⅓ cups orange juice
⅔ cup lime cordial
4 tablespoons dark rum
Dash of Angostura bitters

1. Put the water and sugar into a saucepan and stir over a medium heat
until the sugar has dissolved. Boil for 5 minutes, then remove from the
heat and allow to cool completely.

2. Once the sugar syrup is cold, stir in the remaining ingredients and chill
for 30 minutes.

3. Churn in an ice-cream maker according to the manufacturer's
instructions until set (thick). If not serving straightaway, spoon into
a suitable freezing container until hard (almost at once if making in a
machine, but 5–6 hours if making by hand).

CHOCOLATE GRANITA

This chocolate granita is much lighter than a sorbet. Bear in mind that for best results, you need to stir the granita every hour for 4–5 hours.

SERVES 4–6

3$\frac{1}{3}$ cups water
1$\frac{1}{2}$ cups superfine sugar
$\frac{1}{2}$ cup cocoa powder

1. Place all the ingredients in a saucepan and bring to a boil, stirring, until the sugar has dissolved. Remove from the heat and allow to cool completely.

2. Pour into a large, shallow freezing container and freeze until ice crystals start to form around the edges. Scrape around the edges of the granita with a fork to disperse the crystals. Continue to scrape the mixture every 30–40 minutes for 4–5 hours, until the mixture is firm, but not frozen solid.

3. Soften at room temperature, 5–10 minutes, before serving.

ICE-CREAM TIP
If the mixture freezes solid, take it out of the freezer and leave at room temperature for about 20 minutes. Break up with a fork until the right texture is obtained.

WATERMELON GRANITA

Perfect on a hot summer's day, this is a wonderfully thirst-quenching granita —it is also a startlingly vibrant shade of pink.

SERVES 4

1¼ cups water
⅓ cup superfine sugar
2 cups watermelon flesh,
 seeds removed

1. Put the water and sugar in a saucepan and stir over a medium heat until the sugar has dissolved. Simmer for 10 minutes and then remove from the heat and allow to cool completely.

2. Put the watermelon flesh in a food processor and process until smooth. Pass through a sieve to remove any stray seeds. Stir into the sugar syrup.

3. Pour into a large, shallow freezing container and freeze until ice crystals start to form around the edges. Scrape around the edges of the granita with a fork to disperse the crystals. Continue to scrape the mixture every 30–40 minutes for 4–5 hours, until the mixture is firm, but not frozen solid.

4. Soften at room temperature, 5–10 minutes, before serving.

AVOCADO & CHILI ICE

A sort of frozen guacamole, this is delicious served with a tomato mousse,
or on the side as an accompaniment to ceviche.

MAKES ABOUT 2 CUPS

3 ripe avocados, peeled and
    pits removed
Juice of 1 lime
Pinch of dried red pepper flakes
4–5 drops Tabasco sauce
1 tablespoon mayonnaise
1¼ cups whipping cream
Salt and ground black pepper

1. Put the avocados in a food processor with the lime juice, pepper flakes, Tabasco sauce, and mayonnaise. Process until smooth and scrape into a bowl. Taste and season well.

2. Lightly whip the cream and fold into the avocado mixture. Taste and adjust the seasoning, if necessary.

3. Pour into a large, shallow freezing container and freeze until ice crystals start to form around the edges. Scrape around the edges of the granita with a fork to disperse the crystals. Continue to scrape the mixture every 30–40 minutes for 4–5 hours, until the mixture is firm, but not frozen solid.

4. Soften at room temperature, 5–10 minutes, before serving.

COFFEE GRANITA

A lovely way to get a hit of caffeine, you might serve this granita in coffee cups with a few chocolate-covered coffee beans sprinkled on top.

SERVES 4

½ cup superfine sugar
2 cups hot fresh coffee, made
   from ground coffee beans

1. Stir the sugar into the hot coffee to dissolve. Allow to become completely cold.

2. Pour into a large, shallow freezing container and freeze until ice crystals start to form around the edges. Scrape around the edges of the granita with a fork to disperse the crystals. Continue to scrape the mixture every 30–40 minutes for 4–5 hours, until the mixture is firm, but not frozen solid.

3. Soften at room temperature, 5–10 minutes, before serving.

EARL GREY SORBET

One of the most delicious sorbets to serve on a hot day—occasionally I substitute Lapsang Souchong but the smokiness is not to everyone's taste.

SERVES 4–6

2½ cups water
⅔ cup superfine sugar
4 Earl Grey tea bags
Juice of 2 lemons

1. Bring the water and sugar to a boil, stirring. Boil for 5 minutes and then remove from the heat and add the tea bags. Leave for 10 minutes and then remove the tea bags. Cool completely.

2. Stir in the lemon juice and chill for 30 minutes. Churn in an ice-cream maker according to the manufacturer's instructions until set (thick). If not serving straightaway, spoon into a suitable freezing container and freeze until hard (almost at once if making in a machine, but 5–6 hours if making by hand).

4. Soften at room temperature, 5–10 minutes, before serving.

ROSE WATER GRANITA

Only make this if you can find a natural extract of rose water. Synthetic flavorings on the market bear no comparison.

SERVES 4

1³/₄ cups water
½ cup superfine sugar
3 tablespoons natural extract of rose water (from health food stores and gourmet markets)
Juice of ½ lemon

1. Put the water and sugar in a pan and stir over a medium heat until the sugar has dissolved. Simmer for 5 minutes. Remove from the heat and allow to cool completely.

2. Stir in the rose water and lemon juice. Chill for 30 minutes.

3. Pour into a large, shallow freezing container and freeze until ice crystals start to form around the edges. Scrape around the edges of the granita with a fork to disperse the crystals. Continue to scrape the mixture every 30–40 minutes for 4–5 hours, until the mixture is firm, but not frozen solid.

4. Soften at room temperature, 5–10 minutes, before serving.

ICE-CREAM TIP
On a hot summer's day, try a scoop of this sorbet instead of a refreshing drink. This is also a great way to end a Chinese or Thai dinner when it is not so easy to find desserts that follow well after the strong Asian flavors.

POMEGRANATE SORBET

Out of season, pomegranates can be hard to find and so I make this sorbet with store-bought, cordial-type syrup, not the Middle Eastern syrup for flavoring savory dishes. If the taste sounds too tart for you, add a little more sugar.

SERVES 4–6

2$\frac{1}{2}$ cups water
2 cups pomegranate syrup
    (from speciality stores)
Juice of 1 lemon

1. Mix the water and pomegranate syrup together and stir in the lemon juice.

2. Churn in an ice-cream maker according to the manufacturer's instructions until set (thick). If not serving straightaway, pour into a suitable freezing container and freeze until hard (almost at once if making in a machine, but 5–6 hours if making by hand).

3. Soften at room temperature, 5–10 minutes, before serving.

CHAMPAGNE GRANITA

While it might seem a little decadent to pour champagne into a granita, this makes a lovely pre-dessert course for a grand dinner, or it can be served as part of a cocktail party appetizer.

SERVES 4–6

1 cup water
1 cup superfine sugar
2 cups champagne

1. Put the water and sugar into a saucepan. Bring to a boil, stirring, until the sugar has dissolved. Boil for 5 minutes and then remove from the heat and allow to cool.

2. Pour the champagne into the sugar syrup and chill for 30 minutes.

3. Transfer the mixture to a large, shallow freezing container and freeze until ice crystals start to form around the edges. Scrape around the edges of the granita with a fork to disperse the crystals. Continue to scrape the mixture every 30–40 minutes for 4–5 hours, until the mixture is firm, but not frozen solid.

4. Soften at room temperature, 5–10 minutes, before serving.

ICE-CREAM TIP
Of course Dom Pérignon would be wasted in this recipe! It is always worth finding a good wine supplier with access to reasonably priced bottles of champagne as these are every bit as good, and sometimes better, than the big labels.

PLUM GRANITA

A fruity-tasting granita that works really well if you want to freeze it as popsicles. At step 3, simply pour the sieved mixture into the mold and freeze until hard.

SERVES 4–6

6 ripe plums, about 1lb, rinsed
1¼ cups water
½ cup superfine sugar

1. Halve the plums and remove the pits. Place in a saucepan with the water and sugar.

2. Bring to a boil, stirring, to dissolve the sugar and then simmer for 5 minutes. Remove from the heat and cool.

3. Pass the mixture through a fine sieve and chill for 20–30 minutes.

4. For the granita, pour the mixture into a wide, shallow freezing container, freeze for 1 hour and then scrape around the edges with a fork to disperse the ice crystals. Continue to scrape around the sides every 30–40 minutes for 4–5 hours until the mixture is firm, but not frozen solid.

5. If possible, serve as soon as firm. If not soften the hardened mixture at room temperature, 5–10 minutes, before serving.

LITCHI SORBET

This is a lovely, palate-cleansing sorbet. Make sure you press out as much juice as you can when sieving the litchi puree.

SERVES 4

2 x 1¼lb tins litchis in syrup
½ cup superfine sugar
Juice of 1 lime

1. Drain the syrup into a saucepan and put the litchis in a food processor. Add the sugar and lime juice to the saucepan. Slowly bring to a boil, stirring, until the sugar has dissolved. Simmer for 5 minutes and then remove from the heat and allow to cool.

2. Process the litchis to a smooth puree, then add the cooled syrup and process again.

3. Strain the mixture through a sieve, then pour into an ice-cream maker and churn according to the manufacturer's instructions until set (thick). If not serving straightaway, pour into a suitable freezing container and freeze until hard (almost at once if making in a machine, but 5–6 hours if making by hand).

4. Bring to room temperature, 5–10 minutes, before serving.

CUCUMBER, PIMMS, & MINT SORBET

Summer in a mouthful, this is an unusual sorbet—cucumbers are not usually associated with sweet things but they taste delicious with Pimms and mint.

SERVES 4

2 cucumbers, rinsed, peeled,
   and roughly chopped
2/3 cup superfine sugar
Juice of 1 lemon
4 tablespoons Pimms
1 tablespoon finely chopped
   mint leaves

1. Put the cucumbers and sugar in a food processor and process until smooth.

2. Pour into a fine sieve set over a bowl and extract as much juice as possible. Discard the pulp.

3. Stir in the lemon juice, Pimms, and mint leaves, then chill for 30 minutes.

4. Churn in an ice-cream maker according to the manufacturer's instructions until set (thick). If not serving straightaway, pour into a suitable freezing container and freeze until hard (almost at once if making in a machine, but 5–6 hours if making by hand).

5. If possible, serve as soon as the sorbet becomes hard. If not, bring to room temperature, 5–10 minutes, before serving.

PEACH & ROSEMARY GRANITA

This might seem an odd combination but herbs and fruit go very well together, especially the woodiness of rosemary and the sweet, perfumed peach. This granita looks impressive served in glasses with fancy spoons, decorated with rosemary sprigs.

SERVES 4–6

5 ripe peaches
2 cups water
½ cup superfine sugar
2 rosemary sprigs

1. Plunge the peaches into a saucepan of boiling water, leave for 10 seconds and then plunge into cold water and peel off the skins.

2. Halve the peaches, remove the pits, and put the flesh into a food processor. Process until a smooth puree forms.

3. Put the water, sugar, and rosemary into a saucepan and stir over a medium heat until the sugar has dissolved. Turn up the heat and boil for 5 minutes. Remove from the heat and allow to cool, then discard the rosemary before stirring in the peach puree. Chill for 30 minutes.

4. Pour the mixture into a wide, shallow freezing container, freeze for 1 hour and then scrape around the edges with a fork to disperse the ice crystals. Continue to scrape around the sides every 30–40 minutes, for 4–5 hours, until the mixture is firm, but not frozen solid.

5. Serve at once or freeze until hard, about 5–6 hours. Bring to room temperature, 5–10 minutes, before serving.

NECTARINE GRANITA

You can use white- or yellow-fleshed nectarines. I find the flavor is much the same, but the color of the granita is better with the yellow varieties.

SERVES 4–6

5 ripe nectarines
2 cups water
½ cup superfine sugar

1. Plunge the nectarines into a saucepan of boiling water, leave for 10 seconds and then plunge into cold water and peel off the skins. Halve, remove the pits, and put the flesh into a food processor. Process until a smooth puree forms.

2. Put the water and sugar into a saucepan and stir over a medium heat until the sugar has dissolved. Turn up the heat and boil for 5 minutes. Remove from the heat and allow to cool before stirring the syrup into the nectarine puree. Chill for 30 minutes.

3. Pour into a wide, shallow freezing container and freeze for 1 hour, then scrape around the edges with a fork to disperse the ice crystals. Continue to scrape around the sides every 30–40 minutes for 4–5 hours until the mixture is firm, but not frozen solid.

4. Serve at once when firm or freeze until hard, about 5–6 hours. Bring to room temperature, 5–10 minutes, before serving.

GRAPE SORBET

This is a lovely, light sorbet with a really refreshing flavor.

SERVES 4–6

3 cups organic red grape juice
1–2 tablespoons superfine sugar
   (optional)
1 egg white, lightly beaten

1. Put the grape juice in a saucepan, bring to a boil, and continue boiling for 8 minutes. Remove from the heat and allow to cool completely. Add 1–2 tablespoons sugar at this stage, if you think the syrup lacks a little sweetness.

2. Chill for 30 minutes, then churn in an ice-cream maker according to the manufacturer's instructions until the mixture is just becoming slushy.

3. Pour in the lightly beaten egg white and continue to churn until the mixture has doubled in size. Spoon into a freezing container and freeze hard until ready to serve (almost at once if making in a machine, but 5–6 hours if making by hand).

4. Bring to room temperature, 5–10 minutes, before serving.

ICE-CREAM TIP
The best-tasting grape juice tends to be organic and you can be sure there are no pesticides in it. I buy a particularly sweet one, but if you think the reduced grape juice is not quite sweet enough for your taste, add 1–2 tablespoons superfine sugar.

PARFAITS & SEMIFREDDOS

CHOCOLATE HONEYCOMB PARFAIT

A light parfait with knobs of chocolate honeycomb running through—this is a great pantry dessert that you can quickly make, and then forget about until you are ready to serve.

SERVES 4–6

4 egg yolks
½ cup superfine sugar
3 chocolate honeycomb bars,
   roughly crumbled
1¾ cups whipping cream

1. Put the egg yolks into a bowl with the sugar and beat until pale and bulky, about 8–10 minutes.

2. Fold in the crumbled chocolate honeycomb bars.

3. Lightly whip the cream to soft peaks and then fold into the honeycomb mixture. Freeze in a suitable freezing container or individual glasses until hard, about 5–6 hours.

4. Serve straight from the freezer.

GINGER & LIME PARFAIT

A wonderful zingy parfait—unlike an ice cream, this can be served straight from the freezer so you can pour the mixture into glasses and serve with just a tuile cookie or brandy snap on the side.

SERVES 4–6

4 egg yolks
½ cup superfine sugar
Grated zest and juice of 2 limes
One thumb-size piece of fresh ginger
    root, peeled and finely grated
2 cups whipping cream

1. Put the egg yolks, sugar, grated lime zest and juice, and grated ginger in a heatproof bowl that fits over a pan of barely simmering water.

2. Beat for about 10 minutes until the mixture is very thick and has tripled in size. Pass through a sieve and allow to cool.

3. Beat the cream to soft peaks and fold into the egg mixture. Pour into glasses and freeze until hard, about 5–6 hours.

4. Serve straight from the freezer.

DARK & WHITE CHOCOLATE SEMIFREDDO

This is a real crowd-pleaser and wonderful served with chilled fresh berries

or, to be really indulgent, a dark chocolate sauce.

SERVES 4

3¼oz bittersweet chocolate (80% cocoa solids), roughly chopped

2 tablespoons milk

3¼oz white chocolate, roughly chopped

1 vanilla bean, split lengthwise

4 egg yolks

⅔ cup confectioner's sugar

1¼ cups whipping cream

TIP
When buying white chocolate, look for more expensive brands rather than the white chocolate for children. They have a finer flavor and are less sickly sweet.

1. Put the dark chocolate and 1 tablespoon milk in a heatproof bowl and set over a pan of gently simmering water to melt. Remove from the heat and allow to cool a little. Repeat with the white chocolate.

2. Scrape the seeds from the split vanilla bean into a bowl, then add the egg yolks and confectioner's sugar. Beat until thick and pale and then stir half the vanilla mixture into each of the melted chocolates.

3. Lightly whip the cream to soft peaks, then fold half into the dark chocolate mixture and half into the white chocolate mixture.

4. Alternately spoon into each of the 4 serving glasses the dark and white chocolate. Once you have done this take the end of a spoon and swirl it through the mixture, cover each glass, and freeze for at least 4 hours or until hard.

5. Serve straight from the freezer.

BLACKBERRY PARFAIT

This recipe resembles a simple blackberry fool that has been frozen. Freezing time aside, it is easy to make and will impress everyone who tastes it, especially served decorated with extra blackberries and fresh mint leaves.

SERVES 4–6

3⅓ cups blackberries, rinsed
¾ cup superfine sugar
3 egg yolks
2 cups whipping cream

1. Place the blackberries in a food processor with half the sugar and blend until smooth.

2. Pass the fruit through a fine sieve and press out as much juice and pulp as possible. Discard the seeds.

3. Put the egg yolks and remaining sugar in a bowl and whisk until pale and bulky. Fold in the blackberry puree.

4. Lightly whip the cream to soft peaks then fold into the blackberry mixture. Pour into a freezing container or parfait glasses and freeze until hard, about 5–6 hours.

5. Serve straight from the freezer.

WHITE CHOCOLATE SEMIFREDDO

A delicious alternative to vanilla ice cream that is a treat eaten on its own and served with fresh berries or a berry coulis.

SERVES 4

6¼oz white chocolate, roughly
   chopped
2 tablespoons milk
1 vanilla bean, split lengthwise
4 egg yolks
⅔ cup confectioner's sugar
1¼ cups whipping cream

1. Put the chocolate and milk in a heatproof bowl and set over a pan of gently simmering water to melt. Remove from the heat and allow to cool a little.

2. Scrape the seeds from the split vanilla bean into a bowl and add the egg yolks and confectioner's sugar. Beat until thick and pale and then stir in the cooled, melted chocolate.

3. Lightly whip the cream to soft peaks and fold into the chocolate mixture. Pour into a large freezing container or dariole molds, cover, and freeze for at least 4 hours or until hard.

4. Serve straight from the freezer.

ICE-CREAM TIP
You will find dariole molds in specialty bakeware stores. They are small, metal containers with high sides that slope out at an angle.

MANGO PARFAIT

This is a simple, sweet parfait, made by beating the egg yolks and confectioner's sugar and leaving out the meringue stage, which makes it lighter and less dense. The ripest mangoes have the best flavor. It is delicious served with fresh, ripe mango.

SERVES 4–6

2 ripe mangoes, rinsed, peeled,
  and pitted
4 egg yolks
1½ cups confectioner's sugar, sifted
1 teaspoon vanilla extract
1¼ cups whipping cream

1. Place the mango flesh in a food processor and process until smooth.

2. Put the egg yolks, confectioner's sugar, and vanilla extract in a large bowl and beat until very thick and pale, about 8–10 minutes. Gently fold in the mango puree.

3. Lightly whip the cream and fold into the mango mixture.

4. Pour into a suitable freezing container or parfait glasses and freeze until hard, about 5–6 hours.

5. Serve straight from the freezer.

PUMPKIN SEMIFREDDO

This has rather an unusual flavor, almost like a cold, creamy pumpkin pie.
Don't be tempted to boil the pumpkin, or it will become watery.

SERVES 4–6

2lb pumpkin
1/3 cup demerara sugar
1 teaspoon vanilla extract
4 egg yolks
1/2 cup superfine sugar
1/2 teaspoon ground cinnamon
1 1/4 cups whipping cream

1. Slice the pumpkin in half and scoop out the seeds. Peel the skin and cut into wedges. Place in a steamer and steam for about 30 minutes or until soft.

2. Transfer the pumpkin flesh to a food processor with the demerara sugar and vanilla extract; process until smooth. Allow to cool completely.

3. Put the egg yolks and superfine sugar into a bowl and beat until thick and bulky, about 8–10 minutes. Sprinkle in the ground cinnamon and then fold in the pumpkin puree.

4. Lightly whip the cream to soft peaks and fold into the pumpkin mixture. Pour into a suitable freezing container and freeze for at least 4 hours or until hard.

5. Serve straight from the freezer.

PRALINE SEMIFREDDO

Made in minutes, especially if you buy ready-made praline. The recipe for praline makes much more than you will need here but it is barely worth making less and it keeps well in an airtight jar for about a month. Use extra praline to decorate the semifreddo when serving.

SERVES 6

4 eggs, separated
1/2 cup superfine sugar
2 teaspoons vanilla extract
1 3/4 cups whipping cream
FOR THE PRALINE
1 2/3 cups blanched almonds
1/2 cup superfine sugar
4 tablespoons water
Oil for greasing

1. To make the praline, place the almonds in a large skillet and toast over a gentle heat, turning frequently, for 4–5 minutes until a golden color. Set aside.

2. Put the sugar and water in the skillet and leave the sugar to dissolve over a very low heat.

3. Increase the heat slightly, add the almonds, and cook until the mixture becomes a golden caramel color, about 8–10 minutes. Immediately pour on to an oiled baking sheet and allow to cool and harden.

4. Roughly break up the praline and place in a food processor—keep some aside to decorate, if desired. Pulse until you have fine bread crumbs.

5. For the semifreddo, put the egg yolks, three quarters of the sugar, and vanilla extract in a large bowl and beat until thick and pale.

6. Whip the cream to soft peaks and fold into the egg mixture. Beat the egg whites to stiff peaks, then beat in the remaining sugar. Fold into the egg mixture.

7. Measure out 1/2 cup praline and fold into the semifreddo. Pour into an individual freezing container or large glasses and freeze for about 4 hours or until just hard. Serve straight from the freezer.

ZABAGLIONE SEMIFREDDO

This is basically a variation of the Italian *zabaglione* (whipped-up egg yolks and sherry) recipe that is frozen. It is best eaten on the day it is made.

SERVES 4–6

5 egg yolks
½ cup superfine sugar
5 tablespoons sweet sherry
1 cup whipping cream

1. Put the egg yolks and sugar into a heatproof bowl and beat until thick and bulky, about 8–10 minutes.

2. Pour in the sherry and set the bowl over a saucepan of barely simmering water on a low heat. Continue beating to stabilize the egg mixture, about 15–20 minutes. Remove from the heat and allow to cool completely.

3. Beat the cream until soft peaks form, then fold into the egg mixture. Pour into a suitable freezing container or parfait glasses and freeze for about 4 hours or until just hard.

4. Serve straight from the freezer.

APRICOT SEMIFREDDO

The only way to make this recipe is to use dried apricots that have not been treated with sulfur. They have a rich caramel flavor that the bright orange, processed dried apricots lack.

SERVES 4–6

½ cup dried apricots
4 tablespoons fresh orange juice
4 eggs, separated
½ cup superfine sugar
1¼ cups whipping cream

1. Place the apricots in a bowl and pour over the orange juice. Soak for 1 hour and then place in a food processor and process until smooth. Set aside.

2. Put the egg yolks in a bowl with half the sugar and beat until pale and bulky.

3. Fold in the apricot puree. Lightly whip the cream and fold into the egg and apricot mixture.

4. Beat the egg whites until soft peaks form, then beat in the remaining sugar, a tablespoon at a time. Fold into the apricot mixture, then spoon into a suitable freezing container. Freeze for about 4 hours or until just hard.

5. Serve straight from the freezer.

CARAMELIZED PEAR PARFAIT

This is a very light, subtle parfait. The pears need to be as ripe as possible, so purchase well in advance.

SERVES 4–6

1 tablespoon unsalted butter
$\frac{1}{2}$ cup superfine sugar
4 ripe pears, rinsed, peeled, cored, and quartered
4 egg yolks
1 teaspoon vanilla extract
1$\frac{3}{4}$ cups whipping cream

1. Put the butter and sugar in a skillet and heat gently until the butter has melted.

2. Add the pears and increase the heat. Cook for 5–10 minutes, turning the pears halfway through—both pears and sugar should be a caramel gold color.

3. Allow to cool a little, then spoon the caramelized mixture into a food processor. Process until smooth and then cool completely.

4. Beat the egg yolks, remaining sugar, and vanilla extract until light and fluffy, about 8–10 minutes. Fold into the cooled pear puree.

5. Lightly whip the cream until soft peaks form and then fold into the pear mixture.

6. Pour into a suitable freezing container or parfait glasses and freeze until hard, about 4–6 hours.

7. Serve straight from the freezer.

IRISH WHISKEY CREAM SEMIFREDDO

I have found that even people who are not particular fans of Irish whiskey cream enjoy this delicately flavored semifreddo. This is delicious served with a sprinkling of cocoa and sweet cookies or tuiles.

SERVES 6

4 eggs, separated
½ cup superfine sugar
⅔ cup Irish whiskey cream liqueur (Baileys)
2 cups whipping cream

1. Put the egg yolks and half of the sugar in a large bowl and beat until thick and pale. Fold in the liqueur.

2. Lightly whip the cream until it just holds soft peaks and then fold into the egg mixture.

3. Beat the egg whites until stiff, then beat in the remaining sugar, a tablespoon at a time.

4. Fold into the liqueur mixture and then pour into a suitable freezing container, then freeze until hard, 3–4 hours.

5. Serve straight from the freezer.

HEALTHY & SPECIAL DIETS

PEACH & AMARETTI YOGURT ICE CREAM

As with all fruit-based ices, the success of the dish rests with the ripeness of the fruit. This is a deliciously light ice cream and perfect for those who can't eat semicooked eggs. Greek yogurt is not essential for flavor, but it has a good texture.

SERVES 4–6

3 ripe peaches
½ cup superfine sugar
2 tablespoons peach schnapps
   (optional)
2 cups Greek yogurt
⅔ cup roughly crusched amaretti
   cookies

1. Plunge the peaches into boiling water for 20 seconds, then immediately plunge into cold water to stop them cooking. Peel off the skins, halve, and remove the pits.

2. Put the flesh into a food processor with the sugar and peach schnapps (if using) and process until smooth. Add the yogurt and process for a few seconds until mixed.

3. Churn in an ice-cream maker according to the manufacturer's instructions until set (thick), then spoon into a suitable freezing container and stir in the crushed cookies.

4. Freeze until hard (almost at once if making in a machine, but 5–6 hours if making by hand).

5. Soften to room temperature, 10–15 minutes, before serving.

VANILLA YOGURT ICE CREAM

A really refreshing ice with an intense vanilla flavor that is almost sorbet-like in its lightness. I use a mix of thick Greek and plain whole milk yogurt, but you could use just one type.

SERVES 4

1⅓ cups confectioner's sugar
1¼ cups water
2 vanilla beans
1 cup thick Greek yogurt
1 cup plain yogurt

1. Put the confectioner's sugar and water in a saucepan. Split the vanilla beans down the middle with a sharp knife and scrape the seeds into the saucepan.

2. Stir over a medium heat until the sugar has dissolved, then simmer for 5 minutes. Remove from the heat and allow to cool completely.

3. When cold, remove and discard the vanilla beans and lightly beat in the yogurts.

4. Churn in an ice-cream maker according to the manufacturer's instructions until set (thick), then spoon into a suitable freezing container and freeze until hard (almost at once if making in a machine, but 4–5 hours if making by hand).

5. Soften to room temperature, 10–15 minutes, before serving.

BLUEBERRY & RICOTTA ICE CREAM

This is a little bit lighter than the usual ice and the ricotta gives an interesting, slightly grainy texture. For a lighter ice, use lowfat milk.

SERVES 4–6

1¼ cups milk
⅔ cup whipping cream
3 egg yolks
⅔ cup superfine sugar
3 cups blueberries, rinsed
1 cup ricotta cheese

1. Put the milk and cream into a saucepan and then bring to a boil.

2. Beat the egg yolks and ½ cup of the sugar until light and fluffy, then pour over the hot milk and cream. Stir well, then return to the pan and stir over a gentle heat until the mixture is thick enough to coat the back of a spoon. Remove from the heat and allow to cool completely.

3. Meanwhile, put the blueberries and the remaining sugar in a food processor and process until smooth.

4. When the custard is cold, beat in the ricotta followed by the blueberry puree. Churn in an ice-cream maker according to the manufacturer's instructions until set (thick), then spoon into a suitable freezing container and freeze until hard (almost at once if making in a machine, but 5–6 hours if making by hand).

5. Soften to room temperature, 10–15 minutes, before serving.

LEMON CONDENSED MILK ICE CREAM

This really is child's play to make, yet also incredibly tasty. It has a smoother texture than the custard-based ice creams but if you are pressed for time, this is the one to make.

SERVES 4–6

2²/₃ cups sweetened condensed milk
²/₃ cup whipping cream
Grated zest and juice of
   3 rinsed, unwaxed lemons

1. Put all the ingredients into a bowl, then mix well. Pour the mixture into a freezing container and place in the freezer until hard, about 5–6 hours.

2. Soften at room temperature, 10–15 minutes, before serving.

ICE-CREAM TIP
The flavor of unwaxed lemon zest is more pleasant to eat, but the taste of the lemon itself is not very different.

STRAWBERRY & SOY MILK ICE

If you are intolerant to dairy produce or eggs, this is the ice cream for you. I use fructose, a natural sugar that really brings out the fruitiness in the strawberries (see tip). Of course, you can substitute superfine sugar if you can't find fructose.

SERVES 4–6

3 cups strawberries, rinsed and hulled
6 tablespoons fructose
1½ cups plain soy yogurt

1. Put the strawberries and fructose in a food processor and process to a smooth puree.

2. Stir in the soy yogurt, then churn in an ice-cream maker according to the manufacturer's instructions until set (thick), then spoon into a suitable freezing container and freeze until hard (almost at once if making in an ice-cream maker, but 5–6 hours if making by hand).

3. Soften at room temperature, 10–15 minutes, before serving.

ICE-CREAM TIP
Fructose can now be found in most supermarkets, along with standard sugars and artificial sweeteners. Alternatively, health food stores normally stock it.

BUTTERMILK & LEMON VERBENA ICE CREAM

Buttermilk has a light tanginess that is completely different from yogurt.
Look for dried lemon verbena in health food stores, which is sometimes
known by its French name, *verveine*.

SERVES 4–6

1¼ cups whipping cream
4 tablespoons dried lemon
   verbena leaves
4 egg yolks
1 cup superfine sugar
3 cups buttermilk

1. Put the cream in a saucepan, then bring to a boil. Remove from the heat, add the lemon verbena leaves, and infuse for 30 minutes. Pass through a sieve to remove the leaves.

2. Beat the egg yolks with the sugar until light and fluffy. Pour over the infused milk and return to the pan. Stir over a very gentle heat until the mixture is thick enough to coat the back of a spoon. Cool completely.

3. Stir in the buttermilk, then churn in an ice-cream maker according to the manufacturer's instructions until set (thick). If the ice cream is frozen almost hard, it can be served direct from the bowl.

4. Alternatively, freeze until hard (almost at once if making in a machine, but 5–6 hours if making by hand).

5. Soften at room temperature, 10–15 minutes, before serving.

RHUBARB, HONEY, & CRÈME FRAÎCHE ICE

As rhubarb is very seasonal, I use ready-made rhubarb compôte, usually found with the jellies in the supermarket. You could use canned rhubarb, but adjust the sugar if it is slightly tart.

SERVES 4–6

1²⁄₃ cups rhubarb compôte
2 tablespoons runny honey
1¹⁄₄ cups crème fraîche

1. Mix all the ingredients together in a large bowl.

2. Transfer to an ice-cream maker and churn according to the manufacturer's instructions until set (thick), then pour into a suitable freezing container and freeze until hard (almost at once if making in a machine, but 5–6 hours if making by hand).

3. Soften at room temperature, 10–15 minutes, before serving.

ICE-CREAM TIP

You can use a fat-reduced crème fraîche if you are watching your weight, but the full-fat version gives a more rounded flavor.

MANGO KULFI

I have included a mango kulfi as I think the fruit marries well with the sweetness of the base flavor. A traditional Indian kulfi is a labor-intensive ice because sweetened milk is boiled for a very long time and then reduced to a thick liquid. Here, I use condensed milk, which has the same flavor and texture.

SERVES 4–6

2¹⁄₃ cups sweetened condensed milk

²⁄₃ cup whipping cream

¼ cup caster sugar

2 ripe mangoes, peeled and
    pits removed

1. Put the condensed milk, whipping cream, and sugar in a heavy-based saucepan. Bring to a boil over a gentle heat, stirring constantly (be careful not to burn the base of the pan). Remove from the heat and leave until cold.

2. Transfer the mango flesh to a food processor and process until smooth. Add the cooled milky mixture and process until smooth.

3. Pour the kulfi mixture into a 5-cup pudding basin and cover with plastic wrap (see tip). Alternatively, pour into individual glasses. Freeze for at least 6 hours, or preferably overnight.

4. Soften to room temperature, 10–15 minutes, before serving.

ICE-CREAM TIP
There is no need to line the basin that holds the kulfi. Just cover the mixture in plastic wrap and dip the pudding basin briefly in hot water to unmold for serving.

CRÈME FRÂICHE & RASPBERRY SWIRL ICE

Another egg-free ice, this is a lighter, less rich version of the usual raspberry swirl but no less delicious. I use fructose to sweeten the raspberries, but you could use superfine sugar.

SERVES 4

1¼ cups water
½ cup superfine sugar
1½ cups crème fraîche
1½ cups raspberries, rinsed
¼ cup fructose (or superfine sugar)

1. Put the water and sugar in a saucepan and stir over a medium heat until the sugar has dissolved. Simmer for 5 minutes, then remove from the heat and cool.

2. Once cold, beat in the crème fraîche and chill for 30 minutes.

3. Meanwhile, put the raspberries and fructose into a food processor and process for a few seconds. Pass through a fine sieve to remove the seeds, extracting as much juice as possible. Chill the puree until ready to use.

4. Churn in an ice-cream maker according to the manufacturer's instructions until set (thick), then spoon the mixture into a suitable freezing container and quickly swirl raspberry puree through the ice cream to achieve a rippled effect. Serve direct from the container, if frozen almost hard.

5. Alternatively, freeze hard (almost at once if making in a machine, but 5–6 hours if making by hand).

6. Soften at room temperature, 10–15 minutes, before serving.

GOATS' MILK YOGURT & PASSION FRUIT ICE CREAM

Goats' milk does indeed have a very strong flavor that some people find overpowering, but the addition of the intense flavor of passion fruit mellows the "farmyard" yogurt taste. This recipe is perfect for those who are allergic to cows' milk. As a special treat top with passion fruit pulp.

SERVES 4–6

2 cups goats' milk yogurt
5 ripe passion fruit
¼ cup superfine sugar

1. Put the goats' milk yogurt in a bowl.

2. In a separate bowl, sieve the passion fruit, squeezing out as much juice as possible. Stir in the sugar and then the sweetened juice into the yogurt.

3. Churn in an ice-cream maker according to the manufacturer's instructions until set (thick) and serve straight from the bowl, if frozen almost hard.

4. Alternatively, freeze until hard (almost at once if making in a machine, but 5–6 hours if making by hand).

5. Soften at room temperature, 10–15 minutes, before serving.

BLACK CHERRY & SOY YOGURT ICE

At a push you might make this low-calorie ice with canned black cherries,
but it won't quite have the same flavor as fresh, ripe fruit.

SERVES 4–6

1 cup pitted black cherries
1 teaspoon vanilla extract
¼ cup superfine sugar
2 cups plain soy yogurt

1. Put the black cherries in a food processor with the vanilla extract and sugar, then process until smooth.

2. Stir in the soy yogurt, then churn in an ice-cream maker according to the manufacturer's instructions until set (thick). Serve straight from the bowl, if frozen almost hard.

3. Alternatively, freeze until hard (almost at once if making in a machine, but 5–6 hours if made by hand).

4. Soften at room temperature, 10–15 minutes, before serving.

YOGURT & CARDAMOM ICE

Don't be afraid of using cardamom in sweet dishes. It works wonderfully well, infusing the ice with a delicate, yet unmistakable flavor. Greek yogurt has a higher fat content and gives a softer, richer ice cream.

SERVES 4

1¼ cups water
½ cup superfine sugar
6 cardamom pods, crushed
3 strips of lemon rind
2 cups Greek or whole milk yogurt

1. Put the water, sugar, cardamom pods, and lemon rind in a saucepan and stir over a medium heat until the sugar has dissolved. Simmer for 5 minutes and then remove from the heat and allow to cool completely.

2. Once the mixture is cold, strain through a fine sieve and stir in the yogurt.

3. Churn in an ice-cream maker according to the manufacturer's instructions until set (thick). Serve straight from the bowl, if frozen almost hard.

4. Alternatively, freeze until hard (almost at once if making in a machine, but 5–6 hours if made by hand).

5. Soften at room temperature, 10–15 minutes, before serving.

FROZEN DESSERTS

KNICKERBOCKER GLORY

The name of this sundae originates from its coloring of red-and-white striped layers that resembled girls' stockings in the 1930s. There is no precise recipe—everyone adds their own favorite flavorings—so experiment with different fruits and syrups.

SERVES 4

2 bananas, peeled and finely sliced
1 x quantity Classic Vanilla Ice Cream
   (see page 24)
1 x quantity raspberry sauce
   (see Peach Melba, page 170)
1¼ cups whipping cream
4 candied cherries
4 ice-cream wafers

1. Take 4 sundae glasses and spoon banana slices into the base of each one.

2. Add 2–3 scoops Classic Vanilla Ice Cream to each glass and drizzle over the raspberry sauce.

3. Lightly whip the cream to soft peaks and then spoon over the ice cream. Top each sundae with a cherry and add an ice-cream wafer to each one. Serve at once.

RASPBERRY & MERINGUE BOMBE

This is an easy, though really impressive pudding. Personally, I like the crunch of the raspberry pips, but if you are not of the same opinion then you can pass the raspberries through a sieve and fold in the puree.

SERVES 6

2³/₄ cups raspberries, rinsed, plus extra, to decorate

3 tablespoons framboise (raspberry) liqueur

¹/₄ cup confectioner's sugar

1³/₄ cups whipping or heavy cream

8oz meringues, roughly broken up

1. Put the raspberries, liqueur, and confectioner's sugar in a bowl and mix together, lightly crushing the fruit.

2. Whip the cream to soft peaks (don't overdo this or the texture will be spoiled). Fold in the raspberry mixture, followed by the broken meringues.

3. Spoon into an 8 inch cake pan and gently level out with a spatula. Cover with plastic wrap and freeze until hard, about 3–4 hours.

4. Run a warm cloth around the outside of the cake pan, turn out onto a serving plate and serve at once decorated with extra raspberries.

PEACH MELBA

Named after the Australian opera singer Dame Nellie Melba, the famous chef Auguste Escoffier created this popular dessert in her honor. The raspberry sauce was apparently a later addition.

SERVES 4

1½ cups raspberries, rinsed, plus extra, to serve
¼ cups confectioner's sugar
2 ripe peaches, rinsed
8 scoops Classic Vanilla Ice Cream (see page 24)

1. Crush the raspberries and pass through a sieve, extracting as much juice as possible. Discard the seeds. Stir the confectioner's sugar into the puree.

2. Dip the peaches in boiling water for 10 seconds, then peel off the skins. Halve, remove the pits and cut into slices.

3. To serve, place 2 scoops of ice cream in each serving dish alongside peach slices and whole raspberries. Drizzle over a little raspberry sauce.

ICE-CREAM TIP
Out of the soft fruit season, you could make the raspberry sauce with frozen raspberries, but you might need to add a little more sugar—they can be slightly tarter than the fresh fruit.

CHOCOLATE & CHERRY CHARLOTTE

This is a deceptive dessert as it is very impressive, yet takes little time and effort to make. If you have your own homemade chocolate cake to hand, so much the better, but there are some good ready-made cakes available.

SERVES 6–8

15oz can pitted black cherries in syrup

1lb best-quality bought (or homemade) chocolate marble ladyfingers or plain chocolate sponge cake

1 x quantity Rich Chocolate Ice Cream (see pages 26–27), softened just enough for scooping

1. Line a Charlotte mold or 8-inch-deep cake pan with plastic wrap. Drain the cherries, reserving the syrup.

2. Dip each ladyfinger into the reserved cherry syrup or slice the chocolate cake into fingers (about the same size as ladyfingers), if using, then dip each into the reserved syrup. Line the base and sides of the mold with cake, leaving enough to cover the top.

3. Spoon half the softened ice cream into the base of the mold in an even layer. Cover with the drained cherries.

4. Layer the remaining ice cream over the cherries and top with the reserved fingers of chocolate cake. Cover with plastic wrap and freeze for 2–3 hours until hard.

5. To serve, turn the mold out onto a serving plate and chill for 15–20 minutes to soften slightly. Serve sliced in wedges.

ARCTIC ROLL

The mass-produced arctic roll might have been the staple dessert on every British school menu in the 1970s and has therefore become a bit of a joke, but a homemade arctic roll is absolutely delicious.

SERVES 6–8

1 x quantity Classic Vanilla Ice Cream
  (see page 24), slightly softened
5 eggs
$\frac{1}{2}$ cup superfine sugar
$\frac{3}{4}$ cup all-purpose flour, sifted
5 tablespoons raspberry jelly

1. Take a large piece of plastic wrap and lay it on a large cutting board or work surface. Put the Classic Vanilla Ice Cream in the center and shape into a long cylinder, the same length as the jelly roll pan (see Step 2). Roll up tightly in plastic wrap and freeze for 1 hour.

2. Meanwhile, preheat the oven to 350°F. Line a jelly roll pan, about 10 x 13 inches, with waxed paper.

3. Put the eggs and sugar in a bowl and beat until thick and pale. Gently fold in the flour.

4. Spread the mixture over the waxed paper and bake in the oven for 5–8 minutes until golden in colour and springy to the touch. Allow to cool in the pan.

5. When completely cold, turn out and spread raspberry jelly over the top. Unwrap the ice cream and place in the center of the cake, then bring up the sides to form a smooth join (you may need to trim away a little of the cake so the edges join neatly).

6. Roll the dessert onto a serving plate, with the join underneath. Slice the arctic roll and serve at once.

ICE-CREAM TIP
Arctic Roll may be kept in the freezer for a few days. Use a hot knife to slice through the ice cream to serve.

FROZEN ICE-CREAM TRUFFLES

This is a really lovely way to finish off a meal, either as a light dessert or an after-dinner treat.

MAKES 12

2 cups Classic Vanilla or Coffee Ice Cream (see pages 24 and 32)
4¹/₂oz bittersweet chocolate (70% cocoa solids), roughly broken up
1 teaspoon vegetable oil

1. Working quickly with a melon baller, scoop out 12 balls of ice cream and place on a sheet of waxed paper. Immediately transfer to the freezer for at least 1 hour to harden up.

2. Melt the chocolate in a heatproof bowl set over a pan of boiling water, or in the microwave for 1–2 minutes. Allow to cool a little, then stir in the vegetable oil.

3. Remove the ice-cream balls from the freezer. Quickly spear each one with a toothpick and dip in melted chocolate. Return to the freezer at once to harden up.

4. Once firm, remove from the freezer and serve with the toothpicks.

CASSATA GELATA

Not to be confused with Sicilian cassata, which is a ricotta cake filled with nuts and fruit, this is a frozen ice-cream bombe with a delightful center of whipped ricotta cheese, cream, candied fruits, and amaretti cookies.

SERVES 8–10

1 x quantity Pistachio Ice Cream (see page 63), slightly softened
1 x quantity Classic Vanilla Ice Cream (see page 24), slightly softened
1³/₄ cups ricotta cheese
¹/₂ cup superfine sugar
¹/₂ cup chopped candied fruit peel, such as orange and citron
2 tablespoons finely chopped almonds
¹/₃ cup crushed amaretti cookies
1¹/₄ cups whipping cream

1. Line a 10-cup pudding basin with plastic wrap. Working quickly, spread the softened pistachio ice cream around the base and up the sides in an even layer. Freeze for 1 hour, or until hard.

2. Spread softened vanilla ice cream over the pistachio in an even layer. Freeze for 1 hour.

3. Meanwhile, beat the ricotta with the sugar until light and fluffy. Stir in the candied peel, almonds, and amaretti cookies. Lightly whip the cream and fold into the ricotta.

4. Spoon the mixture into the center of the bombe, leveling out the surface. Cover with plastic wrap and freeze until hard, at least 4–5 hours.

5. To serve, remove the cover and place a large serving plate over the top of the pudding basin. Turn out, remove the basin and peel away the plastic wrap. Serve at once in slices.

BAKED ALASKA

The sponge cake and ice cream can be prepared ahead of time, but once made this dessert must be served at once before the ice cream begins to melt. When covering the cake and ice cream with meringue, be careful not to leave any gaps or the ice cream will seep out.

SERVES 6–8

1 x 7–8 inch baked sponge cake
4 tablespoons strawberry jelly
2 egg whites
Pinch of cream of tartar
$\frac{1}{2}$ cup superfine sugar
1 x quantity Rich Chocolate Ice
   Cream (see page 26)

1. Preheat the oven to 425°F. Put the cake on a baking sheet and carefully scoop out the center with a metal spoon to make a little hollow in the sponge cake, leaving a rim of about $\frac{1}{2}$ inch. Spread with strawberry jelly.

2. Put the egg whites in a clean bowl and beat until stiff peaks form. Add the cream of tartar and beat in the sugar, 1 tablespoon at a time, until the meringue is glossy.

3. Pile scoops of ice cream into the hollow to form a mound. Spread the meringue all over the ice cream and around the edges, working quickly and flicking up with the knife to create little peaks.

4. Bake in the oven for 3–4 minutes, or until the meringue starts to brown. Serve at once.

ICE-CREAM TIP
For a special occasion, buy mini sparklers to stick into the Baked Alaska as soon as the meringue is baked. It makes a very impressive birthday cake for a small gathering.

BANANA SPLIT

This must go down in history as one of the best-loved ice-cream desserts. With homemade ice cream, it is taken to a different dimension. Vanilla and strawberry ice cream are the traditional flavors, but by all means choose your favorite ices.

SERVES 4

4 bananas
4 scoops Classic Vanilla Ice Cream
   (see page 24)
4 scoops Strawberry Soy Milk Ice
   (see page 157)
¾ cup whipping cream
Ice-cream wafers, to serve
Toasted slivered almonds, to decorate
FOR THE CHOCOLATE SAUCE
4½oz bittersweet chocolate
   (70% cocoa solids), broken
   into chunks
2 tablespoons unsalted butter
⅔ cup heavy cream

1. First, make the chocolate sauce. Place all the ingredients in a saucepan and stir over a gentle heat until smooth and glossy. Allow to cool.

2. Peel and slice each banana lengthwise and lay in banana-split glasses. Put a scoop of each ice cream between each banana half.

3. Drizzle over the chocolate sauce. Whip the cream to soft peaks and add a dollop to each dish. Sprinkle with toasted slivered almonds and serve with ice-cream wafers.

COFFEE LIÉGEOIS

This is a sundae for adults—it needs to be made with good-quality espresso coffee. Similar to the Italian *affogato*, it is embellished with whipped cream and must be served at once.

SERVES 4

1¼ cups heavy cream
2 tablespoons confectioner's sugar,
   sifted
1 x quantity Coffee Ice Cream
   (see page 32)
1 x quantity Classic Vanilla Ice Cream
   (see page 24)
4 shots of freshly brewed espresso
   coffee
Lightly toasted slivered almonds,
   to serve

1. Put the cream and confectioner's sugar in a bowl. Lightly whip until the cream is just holding soft peaks and then chill.

2. Add a scoop each of Coffee and Classic Vanilla Ice Cream to 4 sundae glasses. Pour over the espresso coffee.

3. Spoon over the whipped cream and sprinkle with toasted almonds. Serve at once.

HOT FUDGE SUNDAE

This is quite a grownup version of the well-known sundae. I use a mixture of the Chestnut & Marrons Glacés Ice Cream and Classic Vanilla because they complement each other very well. However, Pistachio Ice Cream (see page 63) used in place of Chestnut is also good.

SERVES 6

5½oz bittersweet chocolate
 (50% cocoa solids),
 roughly broken up
¼ cup soft brown sugar
2 cups whipping cream
1 tablespoon unsalted butter
1 tablespoon light corn syrup
3 chocolate brownies,
 roughly crumbled
6 scoops Classic Vanilla Ice Cream
 (see page 24)
6 scoops Chestnut & Marrons Glacés
 Ice Cream (see pages 60–61)
A few toasted chopped nuts,
 to decorate

1. Put the chocolate, brown sugar, $^2/_3$ cup whipping cream, butter, and light corn syrup in a saucepan. Stir over a gentle heat until the chocolate has melted. Bring to a boil and then remove the sauce from the heat. Keep warm.

2. Lightly whip the remaining cream to soft peaks.

3. Divide the crumbled brownies between 6 sundae glasses. Place a scoop each of vanilla and chestnut ice cream on top of each serving and pour over the hot chocolate sauce.

4. Top each sundae glass with a heaped tablespoon of whipped cream, sprinkle with toasted nuts, and serve at once.

AMERICAN PARFAIT

There seem to be many variations to this popular parfait and indeed you could experiment with your own combinations of ice-cream flavors, fruits, and cookies. Try crumbling some biscotti instead of shortbread or butter cookies.

SERVES 4

1²/₃ cups strawberries, rinsed and hulled
2 tablespoons superfine sugar
4 shortbread or butter cookies
8 scoops Classic Vanilla Ice Cream (see page 24)
1/₃ cup finely chopped hazelnuts, toasted
1¹/₄ cups whipping cream
4 candied cherries

1. In a bowl, roughly crush the strawberries with a potato masher or the back of a fork and stir in the sugar.

2. Place the cookies in a plastic bag, seal, and roughly crush using a rolling pin.

3. Take 4 sundae glasses and put a tablespoon of crushed strawberries in the base of each one. Add a scoop of vanilla ice cream and sprinkle with a thin layer of crushed cookies, plus a sprinkling of chopped hazelnuts.

4. Spoon over each one with another tablespoon of crushed strawberries, another scoop of vanilla ice cream, and the remaining crushed cookies.

5. Lightly whip the cream to soft peaks and quickly pile a little over the top of each parfait. Sprinkle with the remaining hazelnuts, top each one with a candied cherry, and serve at once.

INDEX